The Best of Microwave Cooking from

FRIEDMANS

THE MICROWAVE SPECIALISTS

Our Favorite Cooking School Recipes

THE PUBLISHING/MARKETING ORGANIZATION

BENJAMIN

Recipes compiled by Jody F. Heckenlively
Designer: Pam Forde Graphics
Photography: Herrington-Olson

ISBN: 0-87502-134-4
Library of Congress Catalog Card Number: 84-72098

Produced and published by
The Benjamin Company, Inc.
One Westchester Plaza
Elmsford, New York 10523

Contents

The Friedmans Philosophy

When Arthur Friedman opened the first Friedmans Microwave Oven store in Oakland, California, in 1976, quite a few eyebrows were raised. A store selling nothing but microwave ovens? One tiny retailer pitted against all the giant department stores and discount chains?

Well, that store not only survived, it prospered. And today, the over one hundred stores that sprang from the seeds sown in Oakland are still confounding the skeptics. But there is no great mystery behind the Friedmans story. One simple idea lies at the heart of our success — the idea on which Arthur Friedman founded the first store, the idea in which each new member of the growing Friedmans family of stores has been rooted, one simple but powerful concept: *The customer must be satisfied.*

Our relationship with our customers *begins* when they make a purchase. Let's face it — when most people buy a microwave oven, they're not certain how it works and exactly what they'll use it for. Once they've brought the new marvel home and — armed with little more than a Use and Care Manual — have managed to ruin a roast, devitalize the vegetables, or turn a loaf of bread to stone, they usually end up relegating their microwave oven to the humble role of coffee warmer. (And a rather expensive coffee warmer it is at that!)

This all-too-common scenario *can't* happen to a Friedmans customer — because at Friedmans, *we show you how* to use your oven. We inform, we don't just sell. Meeting individual needs — not just selling — is our priority and commitment. And nowhere is that commitment more graphically demonstrated than in our cooking schools.

Open to *everyone* without charge, basic cooking classes held in every Friedmans store give the serious shopper and curious browser alike an "insider's look" at the microwave oven. Our weekly classes provide an unusual opportunity for all who are interested in microwave cooking. In a friendly, informal atmosphere, shoppers enjoy demonstrations by knowledgeable microwave specialists on how the microwave oven works and what it can do (with tasty evidence to prove the point), as well as comparisons and explanations of the features of *all* the major brands. In our "supermarket" of microwave ovens, there is a

4

model the right size for every household, suited to every customer's need, habits, and budget. We are committed to helping our customers select the oven with the features that are just right for them. And we give them 60 days to determine if they have bought the right oven or feel they would like to exchange it (at no extra charge) for a different model.

Our service doesn't end there! Our commitment to our customers lasts a lifetime. Three or four times a week, in every Friedmans store, microwave chefs and store owners conduct cooking classes (free to Friedmans oven customers and totaling 20,000 classes yearly) that not only are great fun, but are designed to make certain our customers learn how to get every possible advantage from the use of their ovens. From following a microwave recipe to converting a conventional favorite; from appetizers to desserts; from casseroles to international cuisine; we cover the fine points of microwave cooking at lively gatherings to which every Friedmans customer has a standing invitation. Our classes cover more than 20 different topics.

Do you have a question about appropriate utensils and cookware? Our complete line of microwave cooking accessories, from all the famous brand name manufacturers, is used in our cooking classes to help you learn which utensils are the best to use in order to obtain perfect results every time you cook. As a

Arthur Friedman

Friedmans friend-for-life, you're entitled to a very special discount on all the carts, cookware, accessories, and cookbooks your heart craves and your kitchen can accommodate.

And there's more — free luncheon demonstrations for church and community groups, full service and 60-day exchange privileges, free "loaners" if there ever is a need for in-shop repair, constant competitive pricing — it's all a part of our commitment to creating the best place in the world to shop for a microwave oven, and to ensuring our customers a lifetime of satisfaction with their purchase.

Lesson Number One

In these few short pages, we can't possibly explain all there is to know about microwave cooking — and, if you're a Friedmans customer, you already know that half the fun of any cooking lesson is the chance to sample the delicious results!

But in this mini-cooking class, we will give you all the information you'll need to get started. And after all, it's only through cooking — through trying the wonderful recipes you'll find here and in other microwave cookbooks, and through creating new "classics" of your own — that you'll discover the full pleasures and advantages of microwave cooking.

First, the Basics

If you've just bought your first microwave oven, you may be wondering exactly what makes it work. Let's get technical for a moment.

All microwave ovens are equipped with a vacuum tube known as a *magnetron* tube, which converts ordinary household electrical current into microwave energy. Microwaves — very short, high-frequency energy waves that are similar to radio waves — are attracted to water, sugar, and fat molecules. When the microwaves make contact with the food in your oven, they cause the food molecules to vibrate billions of times per second. Just as when two sticks are rapidly rubbed together, this friction generates heat. Since the microwaves travel directly to the food without warming the oven cavity, reflecting off metal walls and passing through dishes, no energy is wasted. Food is cooked more efficiently and quickly than in a conventional oven. In fact, food cooked by the microwave method cooks in as little as one-quarter to one-third of the time required to cook food conventionally (some cook even faster). And, because of the short cooking time, foods such as vegetables retain more of their nutrients and their fresh-picked flavor, appearance, and texture than they do when cooked by a more traditional method.

A Supermarket of Selections

Whether you've already purchased a microwave oven, are trying to decide which oven is right for you, or are thinking about trading in your present oven for a new or different model, you may be interested in knowing about some of the options and features available. Many factors should guide you in your selection of an oven, and a talk with a Friedmans microwave specialist, or attendance at a Friedmans brand-comparison and cooking class, can help you sort out which features are most appropriate to your needs. You'll want to consider the size of your household, the size and layout of your kitchen, whether you'll be using the oven primarily to heat and defrost food, for simple cooking, or for preparing full-course meals, and other factors unique to your situation and needs.

Some ovens come equipped with multipower levels for a wide range of cooking options; some have a limited number of selected power levels; some have only one. Your choice depends on your budget and on how you plan to use the oven.

The controls on your oven may be mechanical with a manual timer, or electronic with touch pads that provide the greatest accuracy for short time settings. Again, your needs will determine your selection, and Friedmans specialists will assist you in making your choice.

Different brands of ovens make use of different techniques for distributing the microwave energy inside the oven cavity. Some use a stirrer fan, others use a turntable — each method has its advantages, and your Friedmans microwave specialist can explain the pros and cons of the method used in the model you choose.

Some ovens come equipped with a glass or ceramic tray specially treated to withstand high temperatures (though the oven itself won't get hot, food and utensils may). Other ovens have a ceramic bottom through which the microwaves pass and are reflected off the steel interior walls.

A temperature sensor or probe can be a useful feature for accurate timing of roasts and poultry, or the reheating of soup, casseroles, and beverages. Whether or not you select an oven that is equipped with a temperature probe, you may find a special quick-reading microwave food thermometer to be a useful tool. (Conventional meat or oven thermometers should never be used in the microwave oven.)

With all of these options available, plus others, you should use your individual cooking patterns and space requirements as a guide in choosing the most suitable oven.

Bringing It Home

Before using your new microwave oven, be sure to review the Use and Care Manual. It will provide instructions on how to use your oven and important information such as cooking wattage, or power level. Wattages of microwave ovens vary — if you cook on high, or 100 percent power, in one oven, you may be using a power level of 600 to 700 watts; in smaller ovens, the power level on high may be 400 to 500 watts. In reality, oven wattage is a minor consideration. But it is important to understand that the lower the oven wattage, the less cooking power available, and therefore the more cooking time required.

Because wattage levels vary among oven models, most microwave recipes, like the ones in this book, give a range of cooking times. A typical recipe may instruct you to "cook on high 4 to 5 minutes." You should cook for the shortest time recommended, check the food, and then continue to cook as necessary. If you know the wattage of your microwave oven (consult your Use and Care Manual or ask your Friedmans microwave specialist), you can make your own adjustments. For example, you'll find that many cookbook recipes (like the ones in this book), as well as instructions on packages of frozen food, are designed for ovens with a high power of 600 to 700 watts. If the 100 percent power setting on your oven is less than 600 to 700 watts, you probably will have to increase cooking time slightly. As a rule of thumb, for each 100 watts of cooking power *lower* than the level for which the recipe was designed, add approximately 15 seconds for each minute of cooking time. Remember, in order to be safe, always *undercook* first and then check the food and add cooking time as needed.

The recipes in this book call for settings of 10 percent power, 20 percent, 30 percent, all the way up through high power, or 100 percent. But your oven controls may not use these same terms. If they do not, the chart on page 9 will help you select the right power level for your cooking.

Let's Get Cooking

Most of the techniques used in microwave cooking are the same as the familiar methods you use in conventional cooking. However, because of the unique way in which microwave

Power Level Controls

Our Recipes Use	For a Power Level of	Your Oven Controls Might Read		
High (100%)	600-700 watts	10	Full Power	High
90%	650 watts	9	Reheat	Medium High
70%	400-500 watts	7	Roast or Bake	Medium High or Medium
50%	300-350 watts	5	Simmer or Slow Cook	Medium or Medium Low
30%	200-250 watts	3	Defrost or Simmer	Medium Low or Low
10%	60-100 watts	1	Warm	Low

energy cooks, some methods may be applied somewhat differently. As in all cooking, common sense and experience are your best guides.

Arranging. Microwaves cook from the outside in toward the center. Therefore it's best to arrange food with the thickest parts or cuts at the outer edge of the cooking dish and the thinner parts at the center. When cooking foods of equal size such as meatballs, potatoes, or tomatoes, arrange them in a ring rather than in a row, and leave the center empty. This method allows microwave energy to reach the maximum amount of surface of food, and therefore promotes even, speedier cooking.

Stirring, Rearranging, Turning over, and Rotating. These methods help food cook evenly by aiding the distribution of heat and microwave energy. Although frequent *stirring* is rarely necessary, occasionally you may want to stir casseroles, soup, and other liquids. Always stir from the outside in toward the center. Food that cannot be stirred, such as potatoes or poultry parts, may be *rearranged* in the dish if they seem to be cooking unevenly. Meat such as hamburgers or steaks may have to be *turned over* during cooking to provide even cooking and browning on both sides. Turning food over is particularly important during defrosting. Some baked goods, such as pies and bar cookies, will cook more evenly if the baking dish is *rotated* a one-quarter or one-half turn partway through the cooking time. Casseroles should be covered and cooked on medium power. In some older ovens it is recommended that a rotating turntable be used. Your Friedmans microwave specialist can show you several models of portable turntables.

Shielding. If the thinnest section of a food such as poultry or a roast seems to be cooking more quickly than the thicker portions, you can prevent overcooking by shielding these areas with small strips of aluminum foil. Be sure to keep the foil at least one inch away from oven walls.

Piercing. Foods such as potatoes, "hard" squash, egg yolks, and other whole items with a skin or membrane must be pierced before cooking to allow a vent for steam to escape.

Standing Time. Because food cooks so quickly by the micro-wave method, standing time is important. During standing time, heat from the surface is conducted to the center to allow the food to finish cooking. Let food stand in the oven or place it on a flat, heatproof surface outside the oven — not a cooling rack — for about five minutes or for the time stated in the recipe.

Covering. Food that should be covered when cooked by a conventional method should also be covered when cooked in a microwave oven. Covers keep food from splattering inside the oven, help retain moisture, and speed heating. If the dish you are using has a cover, use it. Otherwise, use waxed paper, paper towels, or paper napkins to cover food loosely. Use top quality plastic wrap that has a high melting point when a tight cover is required. When plastic wrap is used, it is a good idea to make a

10

small vent by turning back one corner of the wrap. This will prevent moisture from building up inside the dish, causing the plastic wrap to burst.

Waxed paper, or a similar loose-fitting cover, should be used for "roasting" or "baking"; plastic wrap, the utensil's lid, or a similar tight-fitting cover for "steaming" or "poaching."

Timing is Everything

You already know that microwave cooking is quick cooking, and if you'll keep this vital factor in mind, you'll get satisfactory results every time you cook. Remember the most basic rule in microwave cooking — *always cook food for the shortest recommended time.* Then check for doneness. It's easy to add additional cooking time, but no one has ever found a way to undo the damage when food has been overcooked in *any* type of oven! As in conventional cooking, certain characteristics of the food being cooked will influence the length of cooking time necessary — all of which is explained in our weekly cooking classes.

Quantity. The common-sense fact that in some cases *more* food may require *more* time to cook is always true in microwave cooking. The same amount of microwave energy is generated whether you cook one potato or four. With the smaller amount, the energy is concentrated on one item; with the larger amount, the energy must be spread out among all the items. A good rule of thumb: When you double a recipe, add slightly less than 50 percent to the cooking time.

Shape, Density, and Size. In both conventional and microwave cooking, small, thin, or porous foods cook more quickly than large, dense foods. Take this into consideration when arranging food in a microwave oven — try to cook foods of similar size and shape together, and arrange foods of different sizes and shapes with the thickest portions placed at the outer edge of the dish and the thinner portions placed in the center.

Height. Areas of food that are closest to the source of energy will cook the most quickly. In most microwave ovens, that means the top of tall food such as a large roast or poultry will tend to cook more quickly than the rest of the food. Two of the cooking techniques described earlier, turning over and shielding, will help ensure even cooking.

11

Microwave Materials Guide

Cookware Materials	Uses	Comments
Metal	Cookware made of metal, even partially, should *never* be used. Metal reflects microwaves; they cannot pass through the utensil to cook the food. Small strips of aluminum foil may be used for shielding (see page 10). Metal TV dinner trays may be used if recommended by the manufacturer (be sure to remove foil covering), but food will cook more efficiently if it is removed from the tray and placed in a microwave safe dish.	Avoid utensils with metallic glazes or trim, twist ties on plastic bags, and frozen food packages with foil lining. Keep all metal at least one inch away from oven walls.
Paper	Paper towels and napkins make good microwave covers to prevent splattering and absorb excess moisture. Paper towels are good for absorbing fat from bacon and sausage. Paper plates and cups are good for heating and serving foods and beverages, but are not good to use for cooking.	Consult manufacturer's recommendations for colored or recycled paper products.
Plastic Wrap	Plastic wrap makes a good tight cover to trap steam. Vent one corner to allow a little steam to escape and prevent plastic wrap from bursting. Puncture plastic cooking pouches to vent steam.	Consult manufacturer's recommendations to be sure plastic wrap is safe to use. Some plastics melt at high temperatures.

Microwave Materials Guide

Cookware Materials	Uses	Comments
Plastic Cookware	Superior defrosting, heating, and cooking results because of highest microwave transmission. Unbreakable and stackable for storage. Ideal for all foods, excellent for freezer and microwave. Many shapes and sizes available, with and without lids.	Some plastics are for heating or defrosting only. Some lids are for storage only. Consult manufacturer's recommendations or ask your microwave specialist which type of plastics will suit your needs.
Pottery and Porcelain	Good utensils for oven-to-table convenience.	Examine for metallic trim. Perform utensil test for metal in glaze (see page 14) before using.
Straw and Wood	Use for quick warming of food such as bread. Will become dry after long-term use.	Avoid items with lacquer or metallic trim. Do not use if wood is still green because green wood will absorb water and the wood will get hot.

Starting Temperature. In all cooking, the temperature at which food is placed in the oven affects cooking time. Food taken from the refrigerator takes longer to cook than food that starts at room temperature. The timing in our recipes is based on food at its usual storage temperature.

Moisture, Sugar, and Fat. Microwave energy is attracted to water, sugar, and fat, so foods high in these elements will cook the most quickly. Be especially careful when cooking foods in which only a portion of the food is high in moisture, sugar, or fat. That portion will cook more quickly than the rest of the food.

Microwave Safe Utensils

All kinds of wonderful new cooking utensils have been especially designed to help you get the most out of cooking with your microwave oven, and you will find them on the well-stocked shelves at Friedmans. Microwave safe, or microproof, plastics vary in price and durability, as well as in shape and use. They can be of tremendous help in all microwave cooking, from defrosting to reheating to cooking. Your microwave specialist can be of assistance in making your selections. You'll also find that many of the nonmetal casseroles, baking dishes, and bowls you've always used in your conventional oven are perfectly safe to use in your microwave oven. To check whether your utensils are microproof, consult the Microwave Materials Guide and the manufacturer's recommendations, or perform this simple test.

Place the utensil you want to check in the oven empty. Place a cup of water in a glass measuring cup beside it. Cook on high one minute. If the utensil feels hot, it is not safe for use in a microwave oven. If it feels warm, it is safe to use for short cooking periods only, such as brief reheating of food. If it remains cool, it is microproof.

When choosing new microproof cooking utensils, remember the shape of the dish is also important. The best cookware to use in microwave cooking is round, oval, or doughnut-shaped. That's because the corners of square or rectangular dishes receive a greater concentration of microwave energy, and food in the corners may overcook. Always try to select a utensil that is the appropriate size for the recipe you are preparing. Food piled high in a dish that is too small will take longer to cook. If the dish is too large, liquids may spread and attract microwave energy, causing slow, uneven cooking.

Defrosting and Reheating

Many people purchase a microwave oven because they have heard of its wonderful speed and convenience in defrosting and reheating food. Defrosting is indeed one of the marvels of the microwave method, and some ovens have programmed or automatic defrost features to make it even easier. Consult your Use and Care Manual and your Friedmans microwave specialist for information on your oven's special features, and follow these tips for best results:

- Most defrosting is done at 30 or 50 percent power, depending on oven wattage.

- A combination of alternating defrosting time and standing time allows food to thaw evenly. Some ovens have a "cycle defrost" feature that will do this automatically.

- Once microwaves have defrosted a portion of a food, they are attracted to that portion. To keep already thawed parts of food from starting to cook, remove thawed portions from the oven or shield them with small strips of aluminum foil. (See tips on foil use, page 10.)

- Most frozen vegetables can be defrosted and heated to serving temperature right in the package. (But be sure to check packages for foil lining.) Puncture plastic pouches to allow steam to vent.

- Remove meat, poultry, and seafood from the package and place in microwave safe utensils for defrosting. Remove package of giblets from poultry, wire twists, and clamps as soon as possible.

- Turn, separate, rotate, or stir food as it defrosts to ensure even thawing.

Reheating leftovers or meals prepared ahead of time is easy, quick, and convenient in a microwave oven. And the results are wonderful! Food retains its taste, texture, and fresh appearance. Leftovers just don't taste like leftovers anymore! You only need to follow these few simple rules for perfect results.

15

- Place the thickest or densest portions of food at the outer edge of the dish or plate and the thinnest portions in the center.

- Most food should be covered during reheating. Waxed paper is a suitable covering to prevent splatters and retain heat, while plastic wrap or a casserole cover will help hold in moisture.

- If your oven has variable power settings, try reheating food on 80 percent power or at an even lower setting.

- Check food halfway through cooking time and rotate the dish one-quarter to one-half turn to ensure even heating.

- A temperature probe or sensor or a microwave food thermometer can be helpful in determining the time necessary to heat food to the exact internal temperature desired.

- Liquid food such as soup, baby food, or stews with gravy should be stirred when they are removed from the refrigerator prior to cooking.

Browning

Some foods, such as small roasts and chicken, cook so quickly in the microwave oven that they don't have time to brown as much as they do when cooked conventionally. Other foods, such as bacon, which has a high fat content, brown and crisp beautifully. Turkey and beef, lamb, and pork roasts that weigh more than two pounds will brown in the microwave oven because they are cooked for more than fifteen minutes.

You can enhance the browning of steaks and roasts in the microwave oven by removing as much of the outer layer of fat as possible before cooking. This will allow more of the microwave energy to reach the marbling (pockets of fat) in the meat and, as this fat comes to the surface, it will help brown the meat. You can also create an attractive browned appearance on meat and poultry by using bottled browning sauces, microwave shake products, soy sauce, dry seasoning mixes, and herbs. To give breads, cakes, and pies a pleasing brown look, try using dark flour, brush with molasses, or sprinkle with dark toppings such as nuts, brown sugar, cinnamon, or nutmeg.

Special microwave browning dishes can be used to sear and brown the surface of meat, poultry, eggs, vegetables, and sandwiches. Be sure to follow the manufacturer's recommendations for the proper use and care of these versatile microwave utensils, or attend one of our special classes that demonstrate how browning dishes are used.

One other tip: To enjoy the speed and convenience of microwave cooking and still serve beautifully browned food, cook the food in your microwave oven and then finish cooking on the grill, under the broiler, in a skillet, or in a preheated conventional oven for a few minutes before serving.

Converting Your Recipes

Once you've tried some of our favorite recipes, you'll want to prepare some of your own old favorites. Converting a recipe designed for conventional cooking takes a little thought and practice, but you'll find that with a few adjustments in ingredients and cooking times, most of your recipes will cook very well in a microwave oven.

A microwave recipe similar to your conventional recipe will provide good guidelines for ingredient adjustments and timing. Most recipes will require only about one-quarter to one-third of their conventional cooking time. Less liquid will be required for microwave cooking, since little evaporation occurs. You may have to reduce seasonings as well because microwave cooking tends to intensify the flavor. Delicate ingredients such as cheese should be added during the last few minutes of cooking if possible.

Please feel free to consult a Friedmans microwave specialist with any questions regarding recipe conversion — whether you are our customer or not.

A Final Note

No one appliance does everything, and there are a few cooking procedures and types of food that simply are not suited for the microwave oven.

Popcorn may be cooked in a specially designed microwave popper — but *never* in a paper bag.

17

Eggs cannot be cooked in the shell — they may burst from a buildup of steam. For best results, cook them in a microwave egg cooker.

Deep-fat frying is neither safe nor efficient in the microwave oven.

Toast, pancakes, waffles, and flaky pastries will not brown or crisp.

Very large quantities, such as a 25-pound turkey or a dozen potatoes, will cook more efficiently in the conventional oven.

Home canning, which requires exact, prolonged high temperatures, *cannot* be done safely in the microwave oven.

Bottles with narrow necks should not be used as cooking utensils — a buildup of pressure may cause them to shatter.

About the Recipes

To our customers, who have been responsible for the continuing growth and prosperity of the Friedmans family of stores, we dedicate this collection of our favorite microwave recipes. Each recipe is a graduate of a Friedmans cooking class and has been sampled, enjoyed, and pronounced excellent by thousands of discriminating customers and friends across the country.

These recipes represent just a sampling of the tremendous variety of foods — from soups and attractive canapés, hearty casseroles, elegant entrées, and colorful vegetable, rice, and potato dishes, all the way to tempting desserts and delectable candies — that you'll soon be preparing quickly, easily, and deliciously in your microwave oven. We hope that you'll enjoy discovering the simplicity and joy of serving up a meal that your family and friends will pronounce worthy of the greatest microwave oven chefs. And we hope that the favorites from our kitchens will soon become your family favorites, too.

Easy Appetizers

From Guy's Lickety-Split Nachos to Teriyaki Drumettes, here's where you'll find eye-catching, tasty tidbits that make any gathering of family or friends a festive occasion. Whether these recipes are served as a first course in a prepared-in-the-microwave banquet or star on their own as party fare, the results are guaranteed to be more than appetizing. And these hors d'oeuvres cook so quickly and easily in the microwave oven that you'll be able to enjoy them along with your guests.

Homemade soup stars in this chapter, too. For a warming meal-starter or a light supper, try our hearty Broccoli Soup. Or add a special microwave touch to your next gourmet dinner with our Cold-as-a-Cucumber Soup. Either way, you'll agree the microwave oven turns hours of work into minutes — with delicious results.

Cold-as-a-Cucumber Soup

Pasadena, California
4 to 6 servings

3 cups sliced peeled cucumber
½ onion, sliced
2 tablespoons butter
1 tablespoon all-purpose flour
¾ teaspoon salt
2 cups chicken broth
Juice of 1 lemon
⅛ teaspoon dry dill
1 cup dairy sour cream
1 cucumber, peeled, seeded, and diced

Combine sliced cucumber, onion, and butter in 2-quart micro-proof batter bowl or measuring cup. Cover with vented plastic wrap and microcook on high 4 to 5 minutes, or until tender. Add flour and salt, stir, cover, and microcook on high 2 minutes. Stir in chicken broth, lemon juice, and dill. Place in container of food processor or blender and process until puréed. Chill. Stir in sour cream and diced cucumber before serving.

Hot Artichoke-Cheese Dip

Monterey, California
6 to 8 servings

1 can (8½ ounces) artichoke hearts packed in water,
    drained
1 jar (6 ounces) marinated artichoke hearts, drained
1 can (4 ounces) diced green chilies
6 tablespoons mayonnaise
1½ to 2 cups (6 to 8 ounces) shredded Cheddar cheese
Tortilla chips to serve

Grease shallow microproof serving dish. Chop artichoke hearts, combine, and distribute evenly in prepared serving dish. Scatter chilies on top and spread mayonnaise carefully over all.

Appetizers

Cover and microcook on high 4 minutes. Reduce setting to 50% power and microcook 8 minutes, or until hot and bubbly. Sprinkle with cheese. Microcook, uncovered, on high 30 to 40 seconds, or until cheese melts. Serve with tortilla chips.

Broccoli Soup

Morton Grove, Illinois
6 servings

3 cups chopped broccoli
2 tablespoons chopped onion
1 tablespoon freshly chopped parsley or
    1 teaspoon dried parsley
1 teaspoon seasoned salt
2 teaspoons chicken-flavored instant bouillon
    dissolved in 1 cup boiling water
2 tablespoons butter
2 tablespoons all-purpose flour
⅛ teaspoon pepper
2 cups milk
Dairy sour cream (optional)

Combine broccoli, onion, parsley, and seasoned salt in 2-quart microproof batter bowl or measuring cup. Pour in chicken bouillon, cover with vented plastic wrap, and microcook on high 4 minutes. Place in container of food processor or blender and process until puréed. Set aside. Place butter in 2-quart microproof batter bowl or measuring cup and microcook on high 30 seconds, or until melted. Stir in flour and pepper. Microcook on high 30 seconds. Add milk gradually, stirring constantly. Cover and microcook on high 11 minutes, or until thickened, stirring every 3 minutes. Add reserved broccoli mixture and stir. Stir in additional milk if soup is too thick. Cover and microcook on high 1 to 2 minutes, or until heated through. Top with sour cream, if desired.

Variation: Substitute fresh asparagus for broccoli.

Chilled Medallions of Chicken Breast

Eugene, Oregon
6 servings

6 chicken cutlets
1 cup ricotta cheese
1 egg
2 tablespoons freshly chopped parsley
Salt and pepper to taste
1 bunch fresh spinach

Cover chicken cutlets with waxed paper and pound until thin. Combine cheese, egg, parsley, salt, and pepper in small bowl. Set aside. Wash spinach well and discard stems. Set aside one-quarter of nicest looking leaves for garnish. Place remaining spinach in microproof bowl, cover with vented plastic wrap, and microcook on high 1 minute. Cover chicken cutlets with flattened cooked spinach leaves. Spread several tablespoonfuls cheese mixture over spinach and roll up cutlets, jelly-roll style. Place, seam-side down, in microproof pie plate. Cover loosely with waxed paper and microcook on high 10 to 12 minutes. Cool to room temperature and place in refrigerator several hours to chill. Cut into ½-inch thick slices and arrange on serving dish. Garnish with reserved spinach leaves.

Tip: Take these with you on your next picnic.

Teriyaki Drumettes

Concord, California
6 servings

⅓ cup soy sauce
¼ cup sugar
2 tablespoons sherry
1 teaspoon minced gingerroot
1 clove garlic, minced
1½ pounds chicken drumettes (about 18 drumettes)
½ teaspoon cornstarch

Appetizers

Place soy sauce, sugar, sherry, ginger, and garlic in 2-quart microproof batter bowl or measuring cup and stir to combine. Place drumettes in 2-quart shallow microproof baking dish. Pour marinade over. Let stand at least 15 minutes, turning drumettes over at least once. When ready to cook, drain off marinade, reserving 2 tablespoons. Place cornstarch in small bowl and stir in reserved marinade. Stir well and drizzle over drumettes. Cover with waxed paper and microcook on high 8 to 10 minutes, or until tender. Serve hot with lots of napkins.

Artichoke Frittata

Fresno, California
8 squares

2 jars (6 ounces each) marinated artichoke hearts
1 small onion, finely chopped
1 clove garlic, minced
4 eggs
¼ cup dry bread crumbs
2 tablespoons freshly minced parsley or
**   2 teaspoons dried parsley**
¼ teaspoon oregano
¼ teaspoon hot pepper sauce
Salt and pepper to taste
2 cups (8 ounces) shredded Cheddar cheese

Drain marinade from 1 jar of artichoke hearts into 8-inch square microproof baking dish. Drain remaining jar and discard marinade. Chop artichoke hearts and set aside. Add onion and garlic to baking dish, cover with vented plastic wrap, and microcook on high 3 minutes. Beat eggs lightly in 1-quart measuring cup. Stir in bread crumbs, parsley, oregano, hot pepper sauce, salt, pepper, cheese, and reserved artichoke hearts. Pour egg mixture into baking dish and stir to blend. Smooth top, cover with vented plastic wrap, and microcook on 50% power 15 to 18 minutes, or until center is set. Let stand, covered. Cut into 1-inch squares and serve warm or at room temperature.

Nacho Platter

San Luis Obispo, California
14 to 18 servings

2½ pounds lean ground beef
½ pound chorizo sausage, casing removed
1 onion, chopped
Salt to taste
Hot pepper sauce or taco seasoning mix to taste
1 can (16 ounces) refried beans
1 can (4 ounces) diced green chilies
2 to 3 cups (8 to 12 ounces) shredded Monterey Jack or
    Cheddar cheese
¾ cup taco sauce
¼ cup chopped green onions
1 cup chopped ripe olives
1 recipe Tony's Guacamole (see page 25)
1 cup dairy sour cream
Tortilla chips to serve

Crumble beef and chorizo into microwave "ground meat cooker." Add onion. Microcook on high 4 minutes, or until meat is no longer pink, stirring after 2 minutes. Drain off fat and season with salt and hot pepper sauce or taco seasoning mix. Spread beans in large round microproof serving dish. Cover with meat mixture and chilies.

Microcook on high 2 to 3 minutes, or until hot and bubbly.* Cover evenly with cheese, drizzle with taco sauce, and sprinkle with green onions and olives. Mound guacamole in center and top with sour cream. Arrange tortilla chips around edge of dish and serve immediately.

* *Tip:* Prepare platter to this point, cover, and place in refrigerator or freezer. When ready to serve, bring to room temperature, uncover, and reheat in microwave oven at 70% power. Complete recipe as directed above.

Appetizers

Tony's Guacamole

10 servings

3 medium-size ripe avocados, peeled, pitted,
    and cut into chunks
½ large onion, chopped
Juice of ½ lemon
2 tablespoons green taco sauce
2 jalapeño peppers, chopped
2 teaspoons garlic powder
Crackers or tortilla chips to serve

Place all ingredients in container of food processor or blender and process until smooth. Serve with crackers or tortilla chips.

Leo's Chopped Chicken Liver

Capitola, California
6 to 8 servings

1 pound chicken livers
1 large onion
3 hard-cooked eggs
3 tablespoons butter or chicken fat
Salt to taste
Cocktail bread or assorted crackers to serve

Wash chicken livers under cold running water. Trim, separate, and pat dry with paper towels. Pierce livers with toothpick to prevent them from exploding and place in 1-quart microproof dish. Cover with tight-fitting lid or vented plastic wrap. Microcook on high 7 to 8 minutes, or until no longer pink. Set aside. Place onion in container of food processor and process until chopped. Add chicken livers and eggs and process until smooth. Place butter in microproof custard cup and microcook on high 40 seconds, or until melted. Pour into chopped liver mixture and mix well. Season with salt. Spoon into serving dish, cover, and place in refrigerator until well chilled. Serve with cocktail bread or assorted crackers.

25

Guy's Lickety-Split Nachos

Fairfield, California
4 servings

4 cups corn chips
1½ cups (6 ounces) grated Cheddar cheese
Picante sauce to taste

Spread corn chips on microproof serving platter. Sprinkle with cheese and drizzle picante sauce over. Microcook on high 1½ minutes, or until cheese is melted. Serve at once.

Chip Beef Dip

Montclair, California
8 servings

1 package (8 ounces) cream cheese
½ cup dairy sour cream
2 teaspoons milk
1 jar (2½ ounces) dried beef, rinsed and chopped
¼ cup chopped green pepper
2 teaspoons onion flakes
¼ teaspoon garlic powder
Pepper to taste
Crackers and assorted raw vegetables to serve

Place cream cheese in 1-quart microproof batter bowl or measuring cup. Microcook on 30% power 30 seconds. Stir in sour cream and milk until smooth. Add dried beef, green pepper, onion flakes, garlic powder, and pepper. Stir well and microcook on 70% power 6 minutes, stirring after 3 minutes. Serve warm or cold with crackers and raw vegetables.

Note: If serving cold, add additional milk as necessary to make dip of spreading consistency.

One-Dish Suppers

What could be simpler or more satisfying than a tasty casserole assembled, cooked, and served in the same dish, and in just a fraction of the time it would take to prepare it the conventional way? This collection of one-dish wonders features some of the traditional old standards, like One-Dish Macaroni and Beef, as well as some zesty new favorites, like our Burrito Casserole and Mexican Manicotti.

Hearty Italian fare is another natural in the microwave oven — or so our cooking school enthusiasts have found. We think you'll agree with them once you've sampled a few of their wonderful offerings. Stuffed Pasta Shells with Tomato Sauce and Pasta Primavera make it so easy to forget your diet — just this once!

Curry Any Way

Aurora, Colorado
4 servings

3 tablespoons butter
¼ cup minced onion
1½ to 2 teaspoons curry powder
3 tablespoons all-purpose flour
¾ teaspoon sugar
¾ teaspoon salt
⅛ teaspoon ground ginger
1 cup chicken or beef broth
1 cup milk
2 cups diced cooked meat or shellfish (chicken, beef,
    lamb, shrimp, etc.)
½ teaspoon lemon juice (optional)
2 cups hot cooked rice or Rice Pilaf (page 74) to serve

Preheat deep microwave browning dish on high 5 minutes. Add butter, onion, and curry. Microcook on high 1 minute. Blend in flour, sugar, salt, and ginger. Microcook on high 30 seconds. Stir in broth and milk slowly. Microcook on high 8 to 10 minutes, or until thickened, stirring every 2 minutes. Add meat and lemon juice and microcook on high 1 to 2 minutes, or until meat is heated through. Serve over hot cooked rice.

Tip: Serve curry with condiments such as chutney, peanuts, diced apple, shredded coconut, raisins, etc.

Poached Eggs

Ukiah, California
1 to 2 servings

¼ teaspoon vinegar
2 eggs
Buttered toast to serve
Paprika to garnish

One-Dish

Place 1 cup hot water and vinegar in 2-cup microproof casserole. Microcook, uncovered, on high 2 to 3 minutes, or until water boils. Break eggs, 1 at a time, into small dish. Prick yolks with toothpick, and slide eggs gently into casserole. Cover and microcook on high 1 minute 15 seconds. Let stand 2 minutes. Remove with slotted spoon and place on buttered toast. Garnish with paprika.

Note: Cook 1 egg on high 1 minute. Let stand 1½ to 2 minutes. Cook 4 eggs on high 2 minutes. Let stand 2 minutes. Alternatively, cook 4 eggs in 2 batches to ensure evenly cooked eggs. If you own a microwave egg cooker, follow instructions on egg cooker instead.

Unstuffed Cabbage

Newark, California
4 to 6 servings

1 pound lean ground beef
2 or 3 Italian sausages, casings removed
1 medium-size head green cabbage, chopped
1 onion, chopped
1 can (8 ounces) sliced mushrooms, drained
½ teaspoon thyme
Salt and pepper to taste
1 can (10½ ounces) tomato soup, undiluted

Preheat 10-inch microwave browning dish according to manufacturer's directions. When preheated, place beef and sausages in browning dish and microcook on high 5 minutes, or until meat is no longer pink, stirring after 2½ minutes. Drain off fat. Layer cabbage, onion, mushrooms, and meat alternately in 3-quart microproof casserole, ending with meat. Stir thyme, salt, and pepper into tomato soup and pour over casserole. Cover with vented plastic wrap and microcook on high 5 minutes. Reduce setting to 70% power and microcook 10 to 12 minutes, or until cabbage is tender.

Ground Beef and
Baked Beans Casserole

Dublin, California
4 to 6 servings

1 pound bacon, diced
1 pound lean ground beef
½ onion, chopped
1 can (28 ounces) baked beans
½ cup dark molasses
½ cup catsup
¼ cup Worcestershire sauce

Place bacon on microwave bacon rack, cover with paper towel, and microcook on high 3 to 4 minutes. Drain and set aside. Place meat and onion in microwave "ground meat cooker" and microcook on high 5 to 6 minutes, or until no longer pink. Drain off fat. Place meat mixture in 4-quart microproof casserole. Add reserved bacon, beans, molasses, catsup, and Worcestershire. Stir well. Cover with vented plastic wrap and microcook on 50% power 30 minutes, stirring every 10 minutes.

One-Dish Macaroni and Beef

Tucson, Arizona
4 to 6 servings

½ pound lean ground beef
1 cup uncooked macaroni
1 can (8 ounces) tomato sauce
1 can (7 ounces) whole-kernel corn, undrained
⅓ cup catsup
1 tablespoon instant minced onion
1 teaspoon brown sugar
¼ teaspoon chili powder
Salt and pepper to taste

One-Dish

Combine all ingredients in 2-quart microproof casserole and mix well. Add 1½ cups water and stir. Cover and microcook on high about 18 minutes, or until macaroni is tender, stirring after 9 minutes. Let stand, covered, 10 minutes. Stir before serving.

Hamburger and Cream Cheese Casserole

Fort Collins, Colorado
4 to 6 servings

1 pound lean ground beef
½ cup chopped onion
½ cup chopped celery
¼ cup chopped green pepper
1 cup sliced mushrooms
1 can (8 ounces) tomato sauce
⅔ cup creamed cottage cheese
1 package (3 ounces) cream cheese, softened
Salt and pepper to taste
2 cups cooked small macaroni or medium noodles
¼ cup dairy sour cream

Place meat, onion, celery, and green pepper in microwave "ground meat cooker." Microcook on high 6 minutes. Add mushrooms and microcook on high 1 minute. Drain off fat. Place meat mixture in 2-quart microproof casserole and stir in tomato sauce, cottage cheese, cream cheese, salt, and pepper. Microcook on 50% power 8 minutes. Add pasta and microcook on 50% power 3 minutes. Stir in sour cream and microcook on 50% power 2 to 3 minutes, or until warmed through.

Tip: To soften cream cheese, unwrap cheese and place on microproof dish. Microcook on 30% power 30 seconds.

Burrito Casserole

Sunnyvale, California
4 to 6 servings

1 pound lean ground beef
1 small onion, chopped
1 can (19½ ounces) chili beef soup, undiluted
1 can (4 ounces) diced green chilies
4 flour tortillas
2 cups (8 ounces) shredded Monterey Jack cheese
1 cup (4 ounces) shredded Cheddar cheese
1 can (4 ounces) sliced ripe olives
1 tomato, cut into wedges

Place meat and onion in microwave "ground meat cooker." Microcook on high 5 minutes, or until meat is no longer pink, stirring after 2½ minutes. Drain off fat and place meat mixture in bottom half of cooker. Add soup and chilies. Stir to combine, cover with vented plastic wrap, and microcook on high 2 minutes. Place 1 tortilla in bottom of 8-inch round microproof cake dish. Spread one-quarter of meat mixture over tortilla and sprinkle with ½ cup Monterey Jack cheese. Repeat layers 3 times. Sprinkle Cheddar cheese on top and microcook on high 5 to 6 minutes, or until heated through. Sprinkle with olives and garnish with tomato wedges.

Dot's Beef Enchilada Casserole

Albuquerque, New Mexico
4 to 6 servings

1 pound lean ground beef
1 medium-size onion, chopped
1 can (15 ounces) pinto beans, drained
½ cup sliced ripe olives
¼ to ½ cup diced green chilies
1 can (11 ounces) enchilada sauce
1 can (8 ounces) tomato sauce
6 corn tortillas, cut into strips
1½ cups (6 ounces) shredded Cheddar cheese

One-Dish

Place beef and onion in microwave "ground meat cooker." Microcook on high 5 minutes, or until meat is no longer pink, stirring after 2½ minutes. Drain off fat, place meat mixture in bottom half of cooker, and add beans, olives, chilies, enchilada sauce, and tomato sauce. Mix well. Microcook on high 4 minutes. Place half the tortilla strips in bottom of 11 x 7-inch microproof baking dish. Cover with half the meat mixture. Repeat with second layer. Sprinkle with cheese. Microcook on high 2 to 3 minutes, or until cheese melts.

Macho Chili Burritos

South San Francisco, California
4 to 6 servings

1½ pounds lean ground beef
1 small onion
2 cloves garlic
1 fresh hot chili
1 can (16 ounces) crushed tomatoes
1 can (6 ounces) tomato paste
2 tablespoons olive oil
2 tablespoons chili powder
1 can (15¼ ounces) kidney beans, drained
8 flour tortillas
1 cup (4 ounces) shredded Cheddar cheese
1 can (4 ounces) sliced ripe olives

Crumble meat in microwave "ground meat cooker." Microcook on high 8 minutes, or until meat is no longer pink, stirring after 4 minutes. Drain off fat. Place onion, garlic, and chili in container of food processor and process until chopped. Add tomatoes, tomato paste, olive oil, and chili powder. Process 30 seconds. Combine meat, kidney beans, and tomato mixture in 3-quart microproof casserole. Cover with vented plastic wrap and microcook on high 10 minutes, stirring after 5 minutes. Divide filling and spread on tortillas. Roll up and place, seam-side down, in 11 x 7-inch microproof baking dish. Sprinkle with cheese. Microcook on 70% power 4 to 6 minutes, or until cheese melts. Sprinkle with olives.

33

Mexican Manicotti

Phoenix, Arizona
2 to 4 servings

½ pound lean ground beef
1 cup refried beans
1 teaspoon oregano
½ teaspoon cumin
1 package (1¼ ounces) taco seasoning mix, divided
8 manicotti shells
1 can (16 ounces) picante or taco sauce
1 cup dairy sour cream
¼ cup finely chopped green onions
¼ cup sliced ripe olives
½ cup (2 ounces) shredded Monterey Jack cheese

Combine beef, beans, oregano, cumin, and half of taco seasoning mix. Mix well. Fill manicotti shells with meat mixture. Arrange in 10 x 6-inch microproof baking dish. Combine picante sauce and remaining taco seasoning mix with 1¼ cups water. Stir well and pour over filled manicotti shells. Cover with vented plastic wrap. Microcook on high 10 minutes, rotating dish one-half turn after 5 minutes. Turn shells over with tongs, cover, and microcook on 70% power 18 minutes, or until pasta is tender. Combine sour cream, green onions, and olives. Spoon down center of manicotti and top with cheese. Microcook, uncovered, on high 2 to 3 minutes, or until cheese melts.

One-Dish

Pasta Primavera

San Rafael, California
6 servings

1 tablespoon vegetable oil
2 teaspoons salt, divided
½ pound spaghetti or linguine
4 cups chopped or small vegetables
    (snow peas, broccoli, asparagus, mushrooms,
    zucchini, tomatoes, peas)
⅓ cup diced cooked meat (salami, pepperoni, prosciutto)
¼ cup freshly chopped parsley
1 clove garlic, minced
¼ teaspoon pepper
2 tablespoons butter
½ cup heavy cream
⅓ cup grated Parmesan cheese

Place 8 cups water, oil, and 1 teaspoon salt in deep 3-quart microproof casserole and microcook on high 9 minutes, or until boiling. Add pasta, cover, and microcook on high 7 minutes. Stir and let stand 3 minutes. Drain and set aside. Place vegetables, meat, parsley, garlic, remaining 1 teaspoon salt, and pepper in 3-quart microproof casserole. Cover and microcook on high 4 minutes. Drain and set aside. Place butter in large microproof serving dish. Microcook on high 30 seconds, or until melted. Stir in cream and cheese. Add reserved pasta and vegetables and toss. Microcook on 70% power 2 to 3 minutes, or until heated through. Serve with additional cheese, if desired.

Stuffed Pasta Shells
with Tomato Sauce

San Francisco, California
8 to 10 servings

Tomato Sauce
4 cups

2 tablespoons olive oil
1 large onion, finely chopped
3 cloves garlic, finely chopped
2 cans (1 pound 12 ounces each) whole tomatoes,
    coarsely chopped
1 cup dry red wine
4 tablespoons tomato paste
1 teaspoon oregano
1 teaspoon basil
Salt and pepper to taste

Place oil in 3- to 4-quart microproof casserole and microcook on
high 1 minute. Add onion and microcook on high 3 to 4 minutes,
stirring after 1½ minutes. Add garlic and microcook on high 2
minutes. Add tomatoes, wine, tomato paste, oregano, basil, salt,
pepper, and ½ cup water. Stir well, cover with vented plastic
wrap, and microcook on high 15 minutes. Reduce setting to 50%
power and microcook 1 hour, stirring every 15 minutes.
Uncover and microcook on 30% power 20 to 30 minutes, stirring
every 8 minutes. If desired, cover with paper towel to prevent
splattering. Use as much sauce as needed with Stuffed Pasta
Shells. Cover and refrigerate or freeze balance.

Tip: Although tomato sauce cannot be microcooked quickly, the
flavor of the sauce makes the cooking time worthwhile.

One-Dish

Shells

1 tablespoon vegetable oil
¼ teaspoon salt
25 jumbo shells

Place 6 cups hot water, oil, and salt in 5-quart microproof casserole. Cover and microcook on high 10 minutes, or until water boils. Add shells, cover with vented plastic wrap, and microcook on 30% power 8 to 12 minutes, or until just tender, stirring after 5 minutes. Drain and rinse under hot running water. Set aside until ready to fill.

Beef Filling

½ pound lean ground beef
1 small onion, chopped
1 clove garlic, minced
1 egg, beaten
1 cup ricotta cheese
½ cup grated Parmesan cheese
Dash nutmeg
Salt and pepper to taste
5 ounces (half of 10-ounce package) frozen spinach,
    cooked and drained (optional)

Place meat, onion, and garlic in microwave "ground meat cooker." Microcook on high 3 to 4 minutes, or until meat is no longer pink. Drain off fat. Place meat mixture in bottom half of cooker and add remaining ingredients. Mix well. Fill cooked shells lightly with meat mixture. Spoon some Tomato Sauce in bottom of 13 x 9-inch microproof baking dish. Place shells in single layer over sauce and spoon sauce over each shell. Cover with waxed paper and microcook on high 3 to 4 minutes, or until hot and bubbly. Sprinkle with additional Parmesan cheese, if desired, and serve with additional Tomato Sauce.

Tamale Casserole

Bakersfield, California
4 to 6 servings

4 cups boiling water
1⅓ cups yellow cornmeal
3 teaspoons salt, divided
1½ pounds lean ground beef
1 cup chopped onions
1 can (16½ ounces) whole-kernel corn, drained
2 cans (4 ounces each) chopped green chilies
1 can (16 ounces) whole tomatoes, drained and chopped
2 cans (4 ounces each) sliced ripe olives
4 tablespoons chili powder (or to taste)
2 tablespoons all-purpose flour
¼ teaspoon cayenne
¼ teaspoon cumin
1 cup (4 ounces) shredded Monterey Jack or
    Cheddar cheese

Combine water, cornmeal, and 2 teaspoons salt in 2-quart microproof batter bowl or measuring cup. Stir well and microcook on high 2 minutes. Lightly grease 13 x 9-inch microproof baking dish and spread cornmeal mixture on bottom and up sides of dish. Set aside. Place meat and onions in microwave "ground meat cooker" and microcook on high 8 minutes, or until meat is no longer pink, stirring after 4 minutes. Drain off fat and place meat mixture in bottom half of cooker. Add remaining 1 teaspoon salt and other remaining ingredients except cheese. Stir well and spoon over cornmeal mixture in baking dish. Cover with waxed paper and microcook on high 12 minutes. Sprinkle with cheese and microcook on 50% power 2 minutes, or until cheese is melted. Let stand 10 minutes before serving.

Main Course Magic

For those who've always believed "you can't cook meat in a microwave oven," we offer tasty evidence to the contrary. Our first exhibit: London Broil, tender, flavorful, and beautifully seared in a microwave browning dish.

Other favorite beef recipes are accompanied by an assortment of uncommonly delicious pork dishes, including our saucy Ham Framboise and colorful Pork Chops with Chinese Vegetables. And if that isn't enough to melt the skeptic's heart, who can resist our Rack of Lamb, dotted with garlic slivers and cooked to succulent perfection beneath a piquant coating of Dijon-style mustard?

You don't have to tell your family and friends how easy it was to bring main course magic to your table!

Pork Chops with Mustard

Overland Park, Kansas
4 servings

4 pork chops (about ½-inch thick each)
4 tablespoons Dijon-style mustard, divided

Preheat microwave browning skillet on high 5 minutes. Place pork chops in skillet, and press against bottom of skillet with spatula. Let stand 45 seconds and turn chops over. Spread 2 tablespoons mustard over chops, cover with browning dish lid, and microcook on 70% power 6 minutes. Turn chops over and spread remaining 2 tablespoons mustard on top. Microcook on high 12 to 14 minutes per pound, or until no longer pink.

Tip: Combine mustard with your favorite jam to add a sweet fruity flavor.

Sweet and Sour Pork

Jenison, Michigan
4 to 6 servings

1½ pounds boneless lean pork cubes
2 tablespoons cornstarch, divided
1 small onion, thinly sliced
1 can (8 ounces) pineapple chunks, undrained
¼ cup firmly packed brown sugar
¼ cup cider vinegar
3 tablespoons soy sauce
1 teaspoon salt
¼ teaspoon ground ginger
1 medium-size green pepper, seeded and cut into strips
Hot cooked rice to serve

Toss pork with 1 tablespoon cornstarch in 2-quart microproof batter bowl or measuring cup. Stir in onion, pineapple chunks with their liquid, brown sugar, vinegar, soy sauce, salt, and ginger. Cover and microcook on 70% power 25 minutes. Stir in remaining tablespoon cornstarch, cover, and microcook on 70% power 5 to 10 minutes. Add green pepper and let stand, covered, 5 minutes. Serve over hot cooked rice.

Main Course

Pork Chops with Chinese Vegetables

Riverside, California
4 to 6 servings

1 box (6¼ ounces) long grain and wild rice mixture
1 can (10½ ounces) mushroom soup, undiluted
1 bag (16 ounces) frozen Chinese vegetables
4 to 6 pork loin chops (about ½-inch thick each), trimmed
"Teri's Browner" to taste
Pepper to taste

Place rice in 2-quart microproof casserole. Stir in soup and 1¼ cups water. Add Chinese vegetables and stir. Arrange pork chops on top with thickest part of chops at outer edge of dish. Sprinkle with "Teri's Browner" and pepper to taste. Microcook on 70% power 26 to 30 minutes, or until no longer pink, rotating dish after 15 minutes.

Ham Framboise

Napa, California
8 to 10 servings

3 pound canned ham
1 package (10 ounces) frozen raspberries
¼ cup firmly packed brown sugar
2 tablespoons Dijon-style mustard
2 tablespoons lemon juice

Place ham in microproof roasting pan and score top in diamond pattern. Place raspberries, brown sugar, mustard, and lemon juice in container of food processor or blender and process until puréed. Spread half of sauce over ham. Cover with vented plastic wrap and microcook on 50% power 30 to 40 minutes, or until microwave thermometer registers 115⁰F. Turn ham over after 15 minutes and baste with remaining sauce. Let stand 5 minutes. Slice ham and spoon sauce into serving dish.

41

Italian Meatballs

Washington, D.C.
4 to 6 servings

1 pound lean ground beef
½ cup grated Parmesan cheese
½ cup dry bread crumbs
1 egg
1 tablespoon onion flakes
½ teaspoon basil
½ teaspoon oregano
⅛ teaspoon garlic powder
Salt and pepper to taste

Combine all ingredients and shape into 1-inch meatballs. Arrange meatballs in microwave "ground meat cooker" and cover loosely with waxed paper. Microcook on high 5 to 7 minutes. Let stand, covered, 3 minutes.

Tip: Serve as appetizers; as a main dish with tomato or spaghetti sauce; or on hard sandwich rolls, topped with cheese.

Meatloaf Au Gratin

Encino, California
4 to 6 servings

½ cup rolled oats
½ cup chopped onion
¼ cup chopped green pepper
1 can (8 ounces) tomato sauce, divided
1 egg, beaten
1 teaspoon chicken-flavored instant bouillon
¼ teaspoon thyme
Garlic powder, salt, and pepper to taste
1¾ pounds lean ground beef
1 cup cheese cubes (½ inch each)
Paprika

Main Course

Combine rolled oats, onion, green pepper, ¾ cup tomato sauce, egg, bouillon, thyme, garlic powder, salt, and pepper. Add beef and cheese cubes, and mix well. Spoon into 6-cup microproof ring mold. Spread remaining ¼ cup tomato sauce over top and sprinkle with paprika. Cover with waxed paper and microcook on high 15 to 17 minutes, draining off juices after 8 minutes. Let stand 5 to 10 minutes.

Pizza Corn Pie

San Jose, California
4 to 6 servings

1 pound lean ground beef
1 can (8 ounces) tomato sauce, divided
½ cup dry bread crumbs
1 teaspoon oregano
½ teaspoon salt
1 teaspoon Worcestershire sauce
¾ cup (3 ounces) shredded mozzarella cheese
½ cup drained whole-kernel corn
1 can (4 ounces) sliced mushrooms, drained
⅓ cup sliced ripe olives

Combine meat, ½ cup tomato sauce, bread crumbs, oregano, salt, and Worcestershire sauce. Spoon mixture into 2-quart microproof ring mold. Smooth top. Spread remaining ½ cup tomato sauce over meat. Sprinkle cheese, corn, mushrooms, and olives on top. Microcook on high 8 to 10 minutes, or until done, rotating dish after 5 minutes.

Flank Steak Bordelaise

Colorado Springs, Colorado
4 to 6 servings

⅓ cup red wine vinegar
¼ teaspoon dry mustard
⅓ cup vegetable oil
1 tablespoon Worcestershire sauce
¼ cup chopped onion
3 cloves garlic, minced, divided
½ teaspoon salt
1 pound flank steak
3 green onions, chopped
4 tablespoons butter or margarine, divided
1 tablespoon all-purpose flour
½ teaspoon thyme
1 can (10½ ounces) condensed beef broth, undiluted
½ cup dry red wine
2 medium-size zucchini, coarsely shredded
2 medium-size carrots, coarsely shredded
⅓ cup chopped walnuts
Salt and pepper to taste

Place vinegar in small bowl. Add mustard and stir until smooth. Add oil, Worcestershire sauce, ¼ cup chopped onion, 2 cloves garlic, and salt. Pour into plastic bag. Add meat, tie bag, and place in large bowl. Refrigerate 6 hours or overnight, turning bag occasionally to distribute marinade. Place green onions and 2 tablespoons butter in 1-quart microproof batter bowl or measuring cup. Microcook on high 1 to 2 minutes, or until tender. Stir in flour and thyme. Add broth and wine, stir well, and microcook on high 16 to 18 minutes, or until reduced to 1 cup. Set aside and keep warm. Preheat 10-inch microwave browning dish on high 6 minutes. Remove meat from marinade. Discard marinade and place meat in browning dish. Press down with spatula. Microcook on high 1 minute. Turn over and microcook on high 3 to 4 minutes, or to desired doneness. Set aside and keep warm. Combine zucchini, carrots, and remaining clove garlic in 2-quart microproof casserole. Micro-

44

cook on high 3 to 5 minutes, or until just tender. Stir in remaining 2 tablespoons butter and walnuts. Season with salt and pepper. Keep warm. Slice steak thinly across grain. To serve, arrange vegetables on serving platter and arrange meat slices on top. Spoon a little sauce over meat and serve remaining sauce separately.

London Broil

Reno, Nevada
4 to 6 servings

1½ to 2 pound beef top round steak for London broil
2 tablespoons mashed garlic

Preheat microwave browning dish on high 8 minutes. Cover steak with garlic purée and place in preheated browning dish. When sizzling stops, turn steak over and microcook on high 7½ to 10 minutes, or to desired doneness.

Rack of Lamb

Lakewood, Colorado
2 servings

1 lamb rib roast (about 2 to 3 pounds)
1 clove garlic, sliced
2 tablespoons Dijon-style mustard

Cut small slits in fat-side of lamb and insert slivers of garlic. Place, fat-side up, on microproof roasting rack in microproof roasting pan and spread with mustard. Microcook on 70% power 7 to 10 minutes per pound, or until microwave thermometer registers 130°F for rare or 170°F for well done. Let stand on heatproof surface 10 minutes before carving.

Pepper Steak

Hayward, California
4 to 6 servings

½ cup vegetable oil
1 teaspoon salt
Pepper to taste
1 pound boneless beef top round or sirloin steak,
    thinly sliced
¼ cup chopped onion
1 clove garlic, chopped
1 green pepper, seeded and cut into strips
1 cup beef broth
2 tablespoons cornstarch
2 tablespoons soy sauce
Hot cooked rice to serve

Preheat bottom half of 10-inch covered microwave browning
dish on high 5 minutes. Place oil, salt, and pepper in browning
dish. Add steak and stir. Microcook on high 2 to 3 minutes, or
until just browned, stirring every 45 seconds. Add onion, garlic,
green pepper, and beef broth. Cover and microcook on high 3
minutes, or until vegetables are tender-crisp. Place cornstarch
in 1-cup measure, add ¼ cup water, and stir until smooth. Stir in
soy sauce. Pour into browning dish and stir. Microcook on high 3
to 4 minutes, or until thickened, stirring every 1 minute. Serve
over hot cooked rice.

Tip: **Never-Fail Rice**
Place 1 cup long grain rice in 2-quart microproof casserole. Add
1¾ cups water and stir. Microcook, uncovered, on high 12
minutes. Fluff with fork and cover. Let stand 5 minutes. Fluff
again and serve.

46.

Poultry Perfection

Poultry has always been one of our most versatile and economical foods. Add to that the speed, simplicity, and enhanced flavor characteristic of the microwave cooking method, and you'll be calling poultry the *perfect* food.

In this chapter, you'll find a collection of poultry recipes that's sure to please everyone at your table. For simple tastes, try our delicate Parchment Chicken. Heartier appetites? Chicken Cacciatore will draw rave reviews. In the mood for flavorful Oriental cuisine? Our Sweet and Sour Chicken, with its chunks of green pepper and pineapple and its perfectly balanced soy ginger sauce, is easy to prepare and so good it's bound to become one of your own family favorites.

We've topped off our selection with a few recipes featuring those other poultry pleasers, turkey and Cornish hens. You'll find they are so juicy, tender, and flavorful when prepared in the microwave oven, you'll soon be wondering why you ever cooked poultry any other way.

Parmesan Baked Chicken

Cedar Rapids, Iowa
4 servings

½ cup butter-flavored cracker crumbs
    (about 12 crackers)
⅓ cup grated Parmesan cheese
1 teaspoon freshly chopped parsley
¼ teaspoon garlic powder
Salt and pepper to taste
6 tablespoons butter
4 chicken cutlets
Paprika

Combine cracker crumbs, cheese, parsley, garlic powder, salt, and pepper in shallow dish. Place butter in microproof pie plate and microcook on high 50 seconds, or until melted. Dip chicken cutlets in butter and roll in cracker crumb mixture. Place in an 11 x 7-inch microproof baking dish, placing meatiest portions of chicken at outer edge of dish. Sprinkle with paprika. Cover with paper towel and microcook on high 8 to 9 minutes. Reduce setting to 50% power and microcook 7 to 8 minutes.

Parmesan Almond Chicken

Santa Maria, California
4 servings

1 cup finely ground toasted almonds
½ cup grated Parmesan cheese
1 teaspoon paprika
Salt and pepper to taste
4 chicken cutlets
Melted butter

Combine almonds, cheese, paprika, salt, and pepper in pie plate or large dish. Brush chicken with melted butter and roll in cheese-nut mixture, covering chicken cutlets completely. Arrange in single layer in shallow microproof baking dish.

48

Poultry

Cover with paper towel and microcook on high 4 minutes. Turn chicken over, cover, and microcook on high 4 minutes, or until chicken is tender.

Chicken Lasagna

Redding, California
6 to 8 servings

1 package (16 ounces) lasagna noodles
1 tablespoon vegetable oil
7 tablespoons butter, divided
½ pound fresh mushrooms, sliced
¾ cup dry white wine, divided
¼ cup all-purpose flour
4 cups half and half
1 teaspoon tarragon
Salt and pepper to taste
4 chicken cutlets, shredded
5 cups (20 ounces) shredded Monterey Jack or
    Swiss cheese

Place lasagna noodles in 13 x 9-inch microproof baking dish. Cover with hot water. Add oil and cover with vented plastic wrap. Microcook on high 14 to 16 minutes, rearranging noodles after 7 minutes. Drain and set aside. Place 3 tablespoons butter in small microproof bowl and microcook on high 1 minute, or until melted. Add mushrooms and microcook on high 3 minutes. Add ½ cup wine and microcook on high 3 minutes. Set aside. Place remaining 4 tablespoons butter in 2-quart microproof batter bowl or measuring cup and microcook on high 40 seconds. Stir in flour. Microcook on high 1 minute, or until bubbly. Stir in half and half gradually. Microcook on high 14 minutes, or until sauce is thick and creamy, stirring every 4 minutes. Add reserved mushroom mixture, remaining ¼ cup wine, tarragon, salt, and pepper. Stir well and microcook on high 3 minutes. Lightly butter 13 x 9-inch microproof baking dish. Layer noodles, chicken, mushroom sauce, and cheese in baking dish and microcook, uncovered, on high 20 minutes.

Sweet and Sour Chicken

Santa Rosa, California
4 servings

½ pound chicken cutlets, cut into small pieces
"Microshake"
1 can (8 ounces) pineapple chunks
1 cup sugar
2 tablespoons cornstarch
⅛ teaspoon ground ginger
1 chicken bouillon cube, dissolved in
    ¼ cup boiling water
½ cup cider vinegar
1 tablespoon soy sauce
1 large green pepper, seeded and cut into
    ½-inch wide strips
Hot cooked rice to serve

Place chicken in small microproof bowl and sprinkle with "Microshake." Microcook on high 3 minutes. Set aside. Drain pineapple chunks and pour syrup into 2-quart microproof batter bowl or measuring cup. Add sugar, cornstarch, ginger, and bouillon, and stir until smooth. Add vinegar and soy sauce. Stir well and microcook on high 3 minutes. Stir in chicken and microcook on high 6 minutes. Add green pepper and pineapple chunks, cover with vented plastic wrap, and microcook on high 3 minutes. Let stand, covered, 5 minutes. Serve over hot cooked rice.

Poultry

Parchment Chicken

Cupertino, California
4 to 6 servings

1 tablespoon soy sauce
1 tablespoon oyster sauce
1 tablespoon sake or dry sherry
1 teaspoon sesame oil
1 teaspoon sugar
4 green onions, thinly sliced
2 tablespoons finely chopped candied ginger
4 chicken cutlets, cut into thin strips
1 package (6 ounces) frozen pea pods, thawed,
    or about ⅓ pound fresh pea pods

Combine soy sauce, oyster sauce, sake, sesame oil, sugar, green onions, and ginger in 2-quart glass bowl or measuring cup. Add chicken to marinade, stir well, and set aside at least 15 minutes. Cut waxed paper into twenty to twenty-five 4-inch squares. Remove chicken from marinade and discard marinade. Place about 1 teaspoon chicken on each square. Break large pea pods into pieces and place 1 or 2 pieces on top of chicken. Fold in corners of waxed paper toward center of square, envelope-style, and place, seam-side down, in single layer on microwave baking sheet. Microcook on high 4 minutes. Rearrange packets if necessary and microcook on high 1 to 3 minutes, or until chicken is tender.

Tip: If candied ginger is not available, substitute 1 tablespoon ground ginger. This dish is a labor of love, but worth it!

Sherried Chicken

Lansing, Illinois
4 servings

4 chicken cutlets, cut into 2-inch slivers
Chicken-flavored "Microshake"
4 tablespoons butter
1½ cups sliced mushrooms
½ cup dry sherry
1 package (⅞ ounce) chicken gravy mix
1 cup dairy sour cream
2 tablespoons freshly chopped parsley
Hot cooked rice to serve

Preheat 10-inch microwave browning dish on high 8 minutes. Sprinkle chicken with chicken-flavored "Microshake." Place butter in browning dish, add chicken, and microcook on high 4 to 6 minutes, stirring every 1½ minutes. Add mushrooms, cover, and microcook on high 4 to 5 minutes. Drain ½ cup liquid from dish into 1-quart microproof batter bowl or measuring cup. Set dish aside and keep warm. Add sherry to liquid in bowl and stir in gravy mix. Microcook on high 2 to 3 minutes. Reduce setting to 30% power and microcook 1 to 2 minutes. Blend in sour cream, pour over chicken, and stir. Microcook on 50% power 2 to 3 minutes. Sprinkle with parsley and serve over hot cooked rice.

Chicken Cacciatore

San Mateo, California
4 servings

2½ to 3½ pound broiler/fryer, cut into serving pieces
1 package (1¼ ounces) onion soup mix
1 can (16 ounces) stewed tomatoes
¼ pound mushrooms, sliced
½ teaspoon rosemary
½ teaspoon basil
Hot cooked noodles or brown rice to serve

Place chicken in 20 x 14-inch browning bag. Add soup mix, tomatoes, mushrooms, rosemary, and basil. Close bag with rubber band or string. Do not use metal tie twists. Shake well and place bag in 13 x 9-inch microproof baking dish. Cut six ½-inch slits in top of bag. Microcook on high 20 to 25 minutes, shaking bag carefully after 10 minutes. Cut bag open, place chicken on serving dish, and spoon sauce over. Serve with noodles or brown rice.

Garlic Lover's Chicken

Morrow, Georgia
6 servings

40 cloves garlic, peeled
⅔ cup olive oil
4 stalks celery, cut into julienne strips
6 sprigs parsley, chopped
1 tablespoon tarragon
¼ teaspoon nutmeg
2 broiler/fryers, cut into serving pieces
Salt and pepper
⅓ cup Cognac

Place garlic in 5-quart microproof casserole and microcook on high 3 minutes. Pour olive oil into casserole and add celery, parsley, tarragon, and nutmeg. Stir well. Season chicken with salt and pepper. Place in casserole and turn chicken pieces in olive oil mixture to coat. Add Cognac and ½ teaspoon salt and turn chicken in mixture again. Cover with tight lid or vented plastic wrap and microcook on high 20 minutes, rearranging chicken after 10 minutes. Reduce setting to 50% power and microcook 40 minutes, or until chicken is tender, stirring every 15 minutes.

Tip: Serve with French bread and lots of napkins. Spread garlic cloves on bread and dip bread in cooking juices.

"Barbequed" Turkey Breast

Mobile, Alabama
6 to 8 servings

6 to 7 pound turkey breast
Garlic powder to taste
Pepper to taste
Barbecue sauce

Sprinkle turkey breast with garlic powder and pepper. Place, skin-side down, on microwave roasting rack placed in micro-proof roasting pan if necessary. Brush generously with barbecue sauce and cover loosely with waxed paper. Microcook on high 15 minutes. Turn turkey breast over and brush generously with barbecue sauce. Cook on 50% power 1 hour to 1 hour 5 minutes, basting every 15 minutes, or until microwave thermometer registers 170°F to 175°F. Let stand, covered, 5 minutes and carve.

Cranberry-Orange Relish

Oakland, California
about 2 cups relish

1 pound fresh cranberries
1 navel orange, peeled (if desired) and chopped
¾ cup sugar, or to taste

Wash cranberries and pick over. Place in 3-quart microproof bowl. Add orange and sugar, stir well, and cover. Microcook on high 9 minutes, stirring every 3 minutes. If desired, place in container of food processor and process to desired consistency. Place in refrigerator to chill until ready to serve.

Poultry

Golden Turkey
Goleta, California

4 tablespoons butter
1 to 2 teaspoons paprika
Salt to taste
1 turkey, cleaned and giblets removed

Place butter in 1-cup microproof measuring cup and microcook on high 40 seconds, or until melted. Stir in paprika and salt. Pat turkey dry with paper towel, tie legs together with kitchen string, and twist wing tips behind back. Brush butter mixture over turkey and place, breast-side down, on microproof roasting rack placed in microproof roasting pan if necessary. Cover loosely with waxed paper. Microcook on high approximately 7 minutes per pound, basting turkey with juices occasionally. Turn turkey over halfway through estimated cooking time. Remove excess juices from roasting pan about every 20 minutes and set aside to make gravy, if desired. Turkey is cooked when microwave meat thermometer inserted in center of inner thigh registers between 180°F and 185°F. Place turkey on carving board and let stand 20 minutes before carving.

Hint: Some parts of turkey, such as wings and breastbone, tend to overbrown during cooking. To prevent this from happening, shield these parts with small pieces of aluminum foil secured with wooden toothpicks three-quarters of the way through cooking.

Cornish Game Hens with Lemon-Caper Sauce

Lakeport, California
4 servings

2 Cornish hens
Pepper, garlic powder, paprika, and "Microshake"
    to taste
2 tablespoons "Bisto Mix"
2 tablespoons lemon juice
2 tablespoons dry vermouth
1 tablespoon drained capers

Sprinkle hens all over with pepper, garlic powder, paprika, and "Microshake." Place, breast-side down, on microwave roasting rack placed in microproof roasting pan if necessary. Cover lightly with waxed paper and microcook on high 7 minutes. Turn hens over, cover, and microcook on high 7 to 8 minutes, or until microwave thermometer registers 175^{0}F to 180^{0}F when inserted. Pour drippings into 1-quart microproof batter bowl or measuring cup. Set hens aside on serving plate and keep warm. Add enough water to "Bisto Mix" to form thick paste. Add to drippings with lemon juice, vermouth, and 2 to 3 tablespoons water. Microcook on high about 2 minutes, or until thickened, stirring every 30 seconds. Stir in capers. Spoon a little sauce over hens, and serve remainder at table.

Treasures from the Sea

Nothing cooks more quickly — with such wonderful results — than seafood cooked in a microwave oven. Fish cooked this way is a moist, tender treat, as you'll soon discover when you sample our Oriental Sole, Red Snapper Vera Cruz, and all the other flavorful fish entrées included in this collection.

Are there any shellfish fans at your table? If so, they'll be pleased and amazed with the microwave oven's special ability to turn out succulent, tender shellfish — and you'll be equally delighted by the speed and convenience with which you can prepare the most elegant seafood entrées. Steamed Clams and Scampi à la Microwave are our variations of old favorites. And for an unusual twist, try Amy's Scallops with Pine Nuts — a beautiful offering of plump, tender scallops topped with a savory pine nut lemon-butter spread that wings from oven to table in just two minutes.

Fish With Mustard And Tomato

Beaverton, Oregon
6 servings

1½ pounds fish fillets (flounder, sole, cod, etc.)
¼ cup Dijon-style mustard
Salt and pepper to taste
2 medium-size tomatoes, sliced
½ teaspoon basil

Place fish fillets in single layer in 13 x 9-inch microproof baking dish. Spread a little mustard on each fillet, sprinkle with salt and pepper, and cover with tomato slices. Sprinkle tomatoes with basil. Cover with vented plastic wrap and microcook on high 6 to 8 minutes, or until fish flakes easily.

Tip: This is a delicious low-calorie dish. For variety of taste and color, alternate tomato and zucchini slices on top of fish.

Oriental Sole

San Diego, California
4 to 6 servings

1 to 1½ pounds sole fillets
2 tablespoons soy sauce
2 tablespoons lemon juice
1 tablespoon catsup
½ teaspoon ground ginger
Orange slices

Place fish fillets in single layer in 13 x 9-inch microproof baking dish. Combine soy sauce, lemon juice, catsup, and ginger in small dish and pour over fish. Place 1 orange slice over each piece of fish. Cover with vented plastic wrap and microcook on high 5 to 7 minutes, or until fish flakes easily.

From the Sea

Fish Fillets with Brown Butter Sauce

Chicago, Illinois
4 servings

½ cup sliced almonds
¼ cup butter
1 pound fish fillets (flounder, sole, cod, etc.)
Salt and pepper to taste

Place almonds on flat microproof dish and microcook on high 3 minutes, stirring every 1 minute. Set aside. Place butter in 1-quart microproof batter bowl or measuring cup and microcook on high 4 to 5 minutes, or until browned. Set aside. Arrange fish fillets in single layer in 9-inch microproof pie plate with thickest part of fillets at outer edge of dish. Sprinkle with salt and pepper. Cover with vented plastic wrap and microcook on high 3½ to 4 minutes, or until fish flakes easily. Sprinkle almonds on top of fish and pour butter over all.

Helene's Lemon Fish

Atlanta, Georgia
4 servings

1 small whole fish (about 1 pound), cleaned and split,
    or 1 package frozen fish fillets, thawed
1 large onion, thinly sliced
2 medium-size fresh tomatoes, thinly sliced
1 or 2 lemons, thinly sliced
Finely chopped fresh parsley

Place fish in 9-inch microproof pie plate. Overlap thin layers of onion, tomato, and lemon slices over fish. Sprinkle with parsley. Cover with vented plastic wrap and microcook on high 5 to 7 minutes, or until fish flakes easily.

Tip: Garnish with additional slices of tomato, lemon, and chopped parsley.

Stuffed Whole Fish

Schaumburg, Illinois
4 servings

2 tablespoons butter
1½ cups finely chopped mixed vegetables
    (mushrooms, green onions, broccoli, carrots, etc.)
½ cup dry bread crumbs
¼ cup grated Parmesan cheese
2 tablespoons dry sherry or dry white wine
½ teaspoon thyme
2 whole fish (about 1 pound each), cleaned
Lemon juice
Salt and pepper to taste
Finely chopped fresh parsley

Place butter in 2-quart microproof batter bowl or measuring cup. Microcook on high 20 seconds, or until melted. Add vegetables and microcook on high 4 minutes. Add bread crumbs, cheese, sherry, and thyme, and stir well. Fill cavities of fish with stuffing and tie securely with kitchen string. Place stuffed fish in 11 x 9-inch microproof baking dish. Sprinkle with lemon juice, salt, and pepper. Cover with vented plastic wrap and microcook on high 10 minutes, or until fish flakes easily, turning fish over after 5 minutes. Sprinkle with parsley.

From the Sea

Red Snapper Vera Cruz
Visalia, California
4 servings

¼ cup butter or margarine
1 small tomato, peeled, seeded, and chopped
½ cup chopped onion
½ cup chopped green pepper
1 clove garlic, minced
3 tablespoons chili sauce
2 tablespoons lemon juice
2 tablespoons drained capers
1 tablespoon freshly chopped parsley
½ teaspoon thyme
Salt to taste
Hot pepper sauce to taste
1 can (4½ ounces) tiny shrimp, drained
¼ cup dry white wine
4 red snapper fillets

Place butter in 13 x 9-inch microproof baking dish. Microcook 1 minute, or until melted. Add tomato, onion, green pepper, garlic, chili sauce, lemon juice, capers, parsley, thyme, salt, and hot pepper sauce. Stir well, cover with waxed paper, and microcook on high 5 minutes, or until vegetables are almost tender. Add shrimp and wine, stir well, and place fish fillets in single layer over vegetables. Spoon some vegetable mixture over fish, cover, and microcook on high 5 minutes. Give dish one-half turn and microcook on high 5 minutes, or until fish flakes easily when tested with fork.

Steamed Clams

Tukwila, Washington
2 servings

12 clams
2 cloves garlic, chopped
2 tablespoons butter
1 tablespoon freshly chopped parsley

Scrub clams and rinse well. Place in 2-quart microproof casserole. Add garlic and butter and cover with vented plastic wrap. Microcook on high 4 to 6 minutes, or until shells pop open. (Discard any clams that do not open.) Sprinkle with parsley and serve at once.

Tip: Be careful not to overcook. Remove clams as soon as they open. Serve with crunchy French bread to sop up delicious juices!

Scampi à la Microwave

Oceanside, California
2 servings

2 tablespoons olive oil
4 cloves garlic, finely chopped
1 pound large shrimp, shelled and deveined
1 tablespoon freshly chopped parsley

Place oil and garlic in 1-quart microproof casserole and microcook on high 1 minute. Add shrimp, cover, and microcook on high 3 to 4 minutes, or until just pink, stirring occasionally. Sprinkle with parsley.

From the Sea

Shrimp Creole

Knoxville, Tennessee
4 servings

½ cup butter
3 tablespoons chopped onion
3 tablespoons chopped green pepper
3 tablespoons chopped red pepper
½ cup sliced mushrooms
¼ cup all-purpose flour
1 can (8 ounces) tomato purée
½ cup dry sherry
½ cup beef broth
1 pound shrimp, cooked, shelled, and deveined
Hot pepper sauce to taste
Hot cooked rice to serve

Place butter in 2-quart microproof batter bowl or measuring cup. Microcook on high 1 minute, or until melted. Add onion, green and red peppers, and mushrooms. Microcook on high 2 minutes. Stir in flour and microcook on high 2 minutes. Add tomato purée, sherry, and beef broth. Mix well. Add shrimp and microcook on 70% power about 6 minutes, or until sauce is thickened and shrimp is hot. Season with hot pepper sauce. Serve over hot cooked rice.

Amy's Scallops with Pine Nuts

Lombard, Illinois
2 servings

½ pound bay scallops
¼ cup butter
3 tablespoons dry bread crumbs
1 tablespoon chopped green onion
1 tablespoon pine nuts
1 tablespoon lemon juice
1 small clove garlic
Salt and pepper to taste
Paprika

Rinse scallops and pat dry. Place in 4 shells or 1½-quart microproof casserole. Place butter, bread crumbs, green onion, pine nuts, lemon juice, garlic, salt, and pepper in container of food processor. Process until well combined. Spoon over scallops and sprinkle with paprika. Cover with waxed paper and microcook on high 2 minutes.

Perfect Companions

These vegetable, potato, and rice dishes are so colorful and tasty, it seems a shame to call them side dishes. But have you ever noticed — sometimes it's the exceptional accompaniments that really make a meal?

Vegetables cook to perfection in the microwave oven, and their seemingly endless variety and versatility is reflected in the delightful assortment of recipes you'll find in this chapter. You may *think* you've tried Rice Pilaf or Sweet Potato Casserole, but you've never tried anything as easy to prepare — or to enjoy — as our versions of these classics. And to further demonstrate vegetables' versatility, we've included some unusual dishes, like our buttery Candied Ginger Carrots, colorful Beet and Roquefort Salad with Walnuts, and tangy Vegetables with Mustard Vinaigrette, guaranteed to add sparkle to any meal.

Beet and Roquefort Salad with Walnuts

Pleasant Hill, California
6 servings

8 to 10 medium-size beets
3 tablespoons red wine vinegar
3 tablespoons olive oil
½ cup walnut halves
¼ pound Roquefort cheese
Freshly ground pepper to taste

Wash beets well and trim off all but one inch at stem and root ends. Place in 2-quart microproof batter bowl or measuring cup. Add ½ cup water, cover with vented plastic wrap, and microcook on high 20 minutes, or until tender. Let stand, covered, 5 minutes. Drain, peel, and cut into julienne strips. Place beets in mixing bowl, add vinegar and oil, and toss gently to coat. Cover and place in refrigerator until almost ready to serve. To serve, toss beets with walnuts and arrange in shallow serving bowl. Allow to return to room temperature. Crumble Roquefort cheese evenly over beets and sprinkle with black pepper.

Tip: Substitute freshly chopped dill for Roquefort cheese.

Green Beans with Bacon Dressing

Palm Desert, California
6 servings

5 slices bacon
2 eggs, beaten
⅓ cup vinegar
3 tablespoons sugar
¼ teaspoon salt
2 cans (16 ounces each) whole green beans, drained

Companions

Place bacon on microwave bacon rack and cover with paper towel. Microcook on high about 5 minutes, or until crisp. Drain ¼ cup drippings into 1-quart microproof batter bowl or measuring cup. Crumble bacon and set aside. Beat eggs, vinegar, ½ cup water, sugar, and salt, and add to drippings. Microcook on 30% power about 8 minutes, or until thickened, beating every 3 minutes. Keep warm. Microcook beans in microproof serving dish on high 3 to 4 minutes. Pour hot dressing over beans and sprinkle with crumbled bacon.

Tip: If fresh beans are available, place 1 pound beans and ½ cup water in 2-quart microproof batter bowl or measuring cup. Cover with vented plastic wrap and microcook on high 8 minutes. Let stand while preparing dressing.

Vegetables with Mustard Vinaigrette

Orland Park, Illinois
4 to 6 servings

5 to 6 cups assorted sliced vegetables
(broccoli, cauliflower, zucchini, Brussels sprouts,
mushrooms, etc.)
5 or 6 sandwich-size "zip-lock" bags
2 tablespoons dry red wine vinegar
2 tablespoons Dijon-style mustard
1 clove garlic
½ teaspoon sugar
½ teaspoon salt
½ cup olive oil

Place 1 cup sliced vegetables in each sandwich bag. Seal bags and microcook on high about 9 minutes, or until vegetables are thoroughly heated but still crisp. Run bags under cold water to stop cooking. Open bags carefully and arrange vegetables on serving platter. Keep warm. Place vinegar, mustard, garlic, sugar, and salt in container of food processor or blender. Process 30 seconds. Add olive oil slowly through feeding tube and process until well blended. Pour over vegetables.

Stuffed Tomatoes

Stockton, California
6 servings

3 large tomatoes, cut in half crosswise
½ cup dry bread crumbs
¼ cup grated Parmesan cheese (optional)
2 cloves garlic, finely chopped
2 teaspoons basil
3 tablespoons olive oil
Salt and pepper to taste

Scoop out and discard centers of tomatoes and place tomatoes, cut-side down, on paper towels to drain. Combine bread crumbs, cheese, garlic, basil, olive oil, salt, and pepper in small bowl and stir until well mixed. Spoon mixture into tomato halves and place, stuffing-side up, in microproof pie plate. Cover with vented plastic wrap and microcook on high 4 to 6 minutes.

Egg Foo Yung

Oxnard, California
4 servings

3 eggs
8 ounces fresh bean sprouts
1 bunch green onions, chopped
¼ cup sliced mushrooms
1 small green pepper, seeded and cut into ¼-inch strips
Soy sauce to taste (optional)
1 tablespoon butter

Beat eggs in 2-quart microproof batter bowl or measuring cup. Stir in bean sprouts, green onions, mushrooms, green pepper, and soy sauce. Microcook on high 2 minutes. Preheat 10-inch microwave browning dish on high 5 minutes. Add butter. When butter is melted, pour egg mixture into browning dish in 2-inch circles. Microcook on high 1 minute, turn patties over, and microcook on high 1 minute.

Companions

Cauliflower Pie

Smyrna, Georgia
6 to 8 servings

1 medium-size head cauliflower
¼ cup mayonnaise
2 tablespoons Dijon-style mustard
½ onion, finely chopped
½ cup (2 ounces) grated Cheddar cheese

Remove most leaves and most of core from cauliflower. (Leave a few small leaves on cauliflower for decoration.) Wrap in waxed paper and microcook on high 6 to 8 minutes, or until just tender. Combine mayonnaise, mustard, and onion in small bowl. Spread over cauliflower. Place cauliflower in microproof serving dish, sprinkle with cheese, and microcook on high 1 to 2 minutes, or until cheese melts. Cut into wedges to serve.

Candied Ginger Carrots

Joliet, Illinois
4 servings

1 pound carrots, peeled and cut into 1-inch lengths
4 tablespoons butter
¼ cup firmly packed brown sugar
1½ teaspoons ground ginger
½ teaspoon caraway seed

Place carrots in 2-quart microproof batter bowl or measuring cup. Add ¼ cup water, cover with vented plastic wrap, and microcook on high 12 minutes, or until tender. Place butter in small microproof bowl and microcook on high 40 seconds, or until melted. Stir in brown sugar, ginger, and caraway seed. Drain carrots and pour butter mixture over. Microcook, uncovered, on high 2 minutes. Serve immediately.

Marge's Stuffed Zucchini

Salem, Oregon
4 to 6 servings

3 medium-size zucchini
1¼ cups crushed saltine crackers
   (about 25 crackers), divided
1 egg, beaten
1 tablespoon butter or margarine, melted
1 small onion, chopped
½ cup (2 ounces) shredded Cheddar cheese
2 tablespoons freshly chopped parsley
1 tablespoon diced pimiento
½ teaspoon salt
Pepper to taste

Pierce zucchini in several places and place in shallow micro-proof dish. Microcook on high 4 to 6 minutes per pound, or until tender-crisp. Slice zucchini lengthwise, scoop out centers, and set zucchini shells aside. Combine zucchini pulp, 1 cup cracker crumbs, and remaining ingredients in bowl. Stir well and spoon into zucchini shells. Top with remaining ¼ cup cracker crumbs. Place stuffed shells, stuffing-side up, in shallow microproof dish. Microcook on 50% power 8 to 10 minutes, or until heated through and cheese is melted.

Spinach Salad

Arvada, Colorado
4 to 6 servings

1 pound spinach
2 eggs
½ pound bacon
⅓ cup cider vinegar
2 tablespoons sugar
½ teaspoon dry mustard
Salt and pepper to taste
½ cup chopped onion

70

Companions

Wash spinach and pat dry. Tear into medium-size pieces and place in salad bowl. Set aside. Crack eggs into small microproof bowl. Pierce yolks with toothpick, cover with vented plastic wrap, and microcook on 90% power 2 minutes. Place in refrigerator to chill. Cut bacon strips crosswise into ½-inch pieces. Place in 1-quart microproof batter bowl or measuring cup. Cover with paper towel and microcook on high 5 to 6 minutes, or until almost crisp, stirring after 3 minutes. Pour ½ cup bacon fat into small microproof bowl. Drain bacon on paper towel and set aside. Add vinegar, 3 tablespoons water, sugar, and mustard to bacon fat. Season with salt and pepper, stir well, and microcook on high 1 to 2 minutes, or until boiling. Dice eggs and add to spinach with onion. Pour dressing over salad and toss gently to mix. Place reserved bacon bits in small microproof bowl and reheat on high 40 seconds, or until hot and crisp. Sprinkle over salad.

Ollie's Butternut (or Acorn) Squash

Modesto, California
2 servings

1 medium-size butternut or acorn squash
2 teaspoons brown sugar
2 teaspoons butter

Cut squash in half lengthwise, remove seeds, and place squash, cut-side down, in microproof dish. (Add 1 teaspoon water if squash is not fresh.) Cover with vented plastic wrap and microcook on high 6 minutes, or until just tender. Turn squash over and score flesh. Place brown sugar and butter in cavity. Cover and microcook on high 2 minutes.

Tip: To make a baked apple quickly and easily, core apple and remove skin around top. Place a little butter and brown sugar inside cavity, stand upright in small microproof dish, and microcook on high 2 minutes per apple.

Potatoes Supreme

Bloomington, Illinois
4 to 6 servings

6 medium-size baking potatoes, unpeeled
2 cups (8 ounces) shredded Cheddar cheese, divided
¼ cup butter
2 cups dairy sour cream
¼ cup chopped green onions
1 teaspoon salt
¼ teaspoon pepper

Wash and pierce potatoes. Microcook on high 20 minutes, or until tender. Set aside to cool. Place 1½ cups cheese and butter in microproof bowl. Microcook on 70% power about 2 minutes, or until melted. Stir in sour cream, green onions, salt, and pepper. Peel potatoes and grate into cheese mixture. Stir well and place in 2-quart microproof baking dish. Smooth top and microcook, uncovered, on 90% power 7 to 9 minutes. Sprinkle remaining ½ cup cheese on top and microcook 2 minutes, or until cheese is melted.

Twice Baked Potatoes

Amarillo, Texas
4 servings

4 large baking potatoes
Salt and pepper to taste
4 tablespoons chopped ripe olives
½ cup diced green chilies
4 to 6 tablespoons heavy cream
1 cup (4 ounces) grated Cheddar cheese, divided
½ cup dairy sour cream

Scrub potatoes and pat dry with paper towels. Cut small deep slit in top of each potato and place on microproof roasting rack. Microcook on high 15 to 20 minutes, or until tender. Let potatoes cool slightly, cut off tops, and carefully scoop out pulp into 2-quart microproof batter bowl or measuring cup. Season inside of shells with salt and pepper and set aside. Mash pulp and stir in olives, chilies, and enough cream to give mixture desired consistency. Season with salt and pepper and stir in ½ cup cheese. Divide mixture equally among shells, mounding filling slightly in center. Sprinkle with remaining ½ cup cheese and place in microproof serving dish. Microcook on 70% power about 5 minutes, or until potatoes are hot and cheese is bubbly. Top each potato with generous dollop of sour cream.

Tip: Combine mashed potatoes with different ingredients such as cooked crumbled bacon, blue cheese or other cheese, diced ham or chicken, chopped onion, or whatever you like.

Sweet Potato Casserole

San Bernardino, California
4 to 6 servings

1 can (1 pound 13 ounces) sweet potatoes, drained
½ cup butter or margarine, melted
3 eggs, beaten
¼ to ½ cup sugar
½ teaspoon baking powder
1 teaspoon vanilla
⅛ teaspoon cinnamon
1 to 2 tablespoons butter or margarine

Mash potatoes in large bowl. Stir in melted butter, eggs, sugar, baking powder, vanilla, and ⅛ teaspoon cinnamon. Pour into lightly buttered 2-quart casserole. Dot with butter and sprinkle with additional cinnamon. Microcook on 50% power 15 to 20 minutes, or until potatoes are firm. Let stand 5 minutes.

Potatoes Boulangere

Traverse City, Michigan
4 servings

4 medium-size potatoes (about 1½ pounds), peeled
    and thinly sliced
1 medium-size onion, thinly sliced
Salt and pepper to taste
2 tablespoons butter

Layer potatoes and onion alternately in oval microproof casserole, sprinkling salt and pepper between layers. Dot with butter. Add 1 tablespoon water and cover with vented plastic wrap. Microcook on high 10 to 15 minutes, or until tender.

Rice Pilaf

North Hollywood, California
4 servings

1 cup long grain rice
1½ cups chicken broth
¾ cup dry vermouth, divided
3 tablespoons butter, diced
½ small apple, finely chopped
1 green onion, thinly sliced
3 tablespoons freshly chopped parsley
1 small carrot, finely chopped
½ cup chopped mushrooms
1 stalk celery, finely chopped

Place rice in 3-quart microproof casserole and microcook on high 4 minutes, or until browned, stirring every 1 minute. Place chicken broth and ¼ cup vermouth in 1-quart microproof batter bowl or measuring cup. Microcook on high 3 to 4 minutes, or until boiling. Add butter and stir. Pour over browned rice and mix well. Microcook on high 9 minutes, stirring after 4 minutes. Add ¼ cup water, remaining ½ cup vermouth, apple, green onion, and parsley. Microcook on high 2 minutes. Stir well and add carrot, mushrooms, and celery. Microcook on high 3 minutes, fluff with fork, and let stand 5 to 8 minutes.

Just Desserts

We could never call a cookbook complete without the kinds of delectable desserts you'll find here. A delicious ending to the perfect meal has never been so easy!

Our sweets selection includes a virtual bakery of wonderful cakes, cheesecakes, pies, nut breads, and cookies. For the chocoholic, there's Rocky Road Chocolate Cake, Chocolate Cheesecake, Chocolate Pie, and more. Fruit fans will be delighted with our Rhubarb Dream and Poached Pears with Chocolate Sauce. And no matter what the occasion, our Strawberry Party Cake, soaked in strawberry syrup and crowned with mounds of creamy pink-and-white topping, will steal the show.

Candy is so easy to make in the microwave oven that you'll soon be able to satisfy every sweet tooth in the family. And what could be sweeter — or more appreciated — than a holiday gift of homemade confections like our peanutty Funny Fudge or buttery Toffee?

Sock-It-To-Me Cake

Kansas City, Missouri
10 to 12 servings

Filling

½ cup finely chopped pecans
2 tablespoons brown sugar
2 teaspoons cinnamon
12 single graham crackers or vanilla wafers, crushed

Cake

1 package (18¼ ounces) yellow cake mix
1 cup dairy sour cream
½ cup vegetable oil
4 eggs

Glaze (optional)

1 cup confectioners sugar
2 tablespoons milk
1 teaspoon vanilla

Lightly grease 12-cup microwave Bundt pan. Place pecans, brown sugar, and cinnamon in small bowl, and mix well. Combine one-quarter of filling mixture with cookie crumbs. Mix well and use to dust inside of cake pan. Combine cake mix, sour cream, oil, ¼ cup water, and eggs in large mixing bowl and beat according to package instructions. Pour half of batter into prepared pan. Sprinkle half of remaining filling mixture over. Pour remaining batter on top and sprinkle with remaining filling mixture. Microcook on 30% power 11 minutes. Increase setting to high and microcook 5 minutes, or until cake pulls away from sides of pan. Cool in pan on heatproof surface 10 minutes. Invert onto serving plate and let cool completely. Place confectioners sugar in small bowl. Stir in milk and vanilla until smooth. Spoon over cake.

Desserts

Rocky Road Chocolate Cake

Memphis, Tennessee
10 to 12 servings

Cake

Sugar for dusting
1 package (18¼ ounces) devil's food cake mix
⅓ cup oil
3 eggs
1 package (6 ounces) semisweet chocolate morsels
1 cup miniature marshmallows
½ cup chopped nuts (optional)

Chocolate Glaze (optional)

1 cup confectioners sugar
2 tablespoons unsweetened cocoa powder
2 tablespoons butter or margarine, softened
2 teaspoons vanilla

Lightly grease 12-cup microwave Bundt pan and dust with sugar. Place cake mix, 1 cup water, oil, and eggs in large mixer bowl and beat 2 minutes at high speed. Fold in chocolate morsels, marshmallows, and nuts. Pour into prepared pan. Microcook on 30% power 11 minutes. Increase setting to high and microcook 5 minutes. Rotate pan after 2½ minutes if necessary. Cool in pan 10 minutes, then turn out onto serving plate and cool completely. Stir sugar and cocoa in medium-size bowl. Add butter, vanilla, and 2 to 3 tablespoons warm water, and beat until smooth. Spoon over cake, if desired.

Tip: For a special treat, serve with Chocolate Sauce (page 87, "Poached Pears with Chocolate Sauce"). For an extra special treat, throw caution to the winds and serve whipped cream, too!

Creamy Cheesecake

Saginaw, Michigan
6 to 8 servings

¼ cup butter or margarine
1 cup graham cracker crumbs
2 tablespoons all-purpose flour
2 tablespoons sugar
¼ teaspoon cinnamon
2 packages (8 ounces each) cream cheese
1 can (14 ounces) sweetened condensed milk
2 eggs
2 teaspoons vanilla
¼ teaspoon salt

Place butter in 9-inch microproof pie plate and microcook on high 40 seconds, or until melted. Stir in cracker crumbs, flour, sugar, and cinnamon. Press mixture evenly onto bottom and up sides of pie plate. Place cream cheese in 2-quart microproof batter bowl or measuring cup and microcook on 10% power 8 to 9 minutes to soften. Beat with electric mixer until light and fluffy. Beat in milk, eggs, vanilla, and salt until well combined. Pour into crust and microcook on 70% power 18 minutes, or until almost set in center. Chill 2 to 3 hours before serving.

Chocolate Cheesecake

Arlington Heights, Illinois
8 to 10 servings

¼ cup butter
1¼ cups fine zwieback crumbs
1 cup plus 1 tablespoon sugar, divided
1 package (12 ounces) chocolate morsels
½ cup strong coffee
2 packages (8 ounces each) cream cheese, softened
4 eggs
2 teaspoons vanilla
¼ teaspoon salt
1 cup whipped cream (optional)

Desserts

Place butter in 9-inch microproof pie plate and microcook on high 40 seconds, or until melted. Combine half of zwieback crumbs with 1 tablespoon sugar. Stir into butter. Press mixture evenly onto bottom and up sides of pie plate. Place chocolate morsels and coffee in small microproof bowl and microcook on high 2 minutes. Stir well and set aside to cool. Beat cream cheese until fluffy. Gradually beat in remaining 1 cup sugar. Beat in eggs, 1 at a time. Add chocolate-coffee mixture, vanilla, and salt, and beat until well combined. Pour into crust and microcook on 70% power about 18 minutes. Chill 2 to 3 hours before serving. Cover with whipped cream before serving, if desired.

Pumpkin Cheese Pie

Orange, California
6 to 8 servings

2 tablespoons butter
1 cup graham cracker crumbs
⅔ cup plus 4 tablespoons sugar, divided
1 package (8 ounces) cream cheese
3 eggs, beaten
1 can (29 ounces) pumpkin
2 teaspoons pumpkin pie spice
1 cup dairy sour cream
¼ teaspoon lemon peel

Place butter in 8-inch microproof pie plate and microcook on high 30 seconds, or until melted. Stir in graham cracker crumbs and 2 tablespoons sugar. Press onto bottom and up sides of pie plate. Microcook on high 1½ minutes. Set aside. Place cream cheese in 1-quart microproof batter bowl or measuring cup and microcook on high 1 minute to soften. Add eggs, ⅔ cup sugar, pumpkin, and pumpkin pie spice, and mix well. Pour into crust and microcook on high 5 minutes. Reduce setting to 90% power and microcook 12 to 15 minutes, or until center is set. Place sour cream, remaining 2 tablespoons sugar, and lemon peel in medium-size microproof bowl. Mix well and spread over pie. Microcook on high 2 minutes. Place in refrigerator until well chilled. Serve cold.

Pumpkin Spice Cake

Medford, Oregon
6 to 8 servings

Cake

1 cup granulated sugar
2 eggs
1 cup vegetable oil
1 cup canned pumpkin
1½ cups sifted all-purpose flour
1 tablespoon pumpkin pie spice
½ teaspoon baking soda
½ teaspoon salt

Topping

¼ cup all-purpose flour
¼ cup firmly packed brown sugar
3 tablespoons butter, softened
½ cup finely chopped nuts

Beat granulated sugar and eggs together until smooth. Add oil and pumpkin and mix well. Combine 1½ cups flour, pumpkin pie spice, baking soda, and salt, and add to liquid mixture, mixing well. Pour into ungreased 8-inch microproof cake pan. Mix ¼ cup flour and brown sugar. Cut in butter until mixture resembles coarse crumbs. Stir in nuts and sprinkle evenly over batter. Microcook on 50% power 9 minutes. Increase setting to high and microcook 5 to 6 minutes. Cool in pan on heatproof surface 10 minutes.

Desserts

Pumpkin Roll

Palo Alto, California
6 to 8 servings

3 eggs
1 cup granulated sugar
⅔ cup canned pumpkin
1 teaspoon lemon juice
¾ cup all-purpose flour
2 teaspoons cinnamon
1 teaspoon baking powder
1 teaspoon ground ginger
½ teaspoon nutmeg
½ teaspoon salt
1 cup chopped walnuts
2 packages (3 ounces each) cream cheese, softened
¼ cup butter, diced
1 cup confectioners sugar
½ teaspoon vanilla

Line microproof baking sheet with waxed paper. Place eggs in container of food processor and process 35 seconds, or until lemon-colored. With machine running, add granulated sugar and process until slightly thickened. Add pumpkin and lemon juice, and process just until mixed. Combine flour, cinnamon, baking powder, ginger, nutmeg, and salt. Add to food processor and process until well blended. Spread batter on prepared baking sheet. Sprinkle with walnuts and microcook on high 5 to 7 minutes, or until top is almost dry. Sprinkle clean dish towel lightly with confectioners sugar. Invert Pumpkin Roll onto towel. Starting at narrow end, roll cake and towel together, jelly-roll style. Cool, seam-side down, on wire rack. Place cream cheese and butter in container of food processor and process until smooth. Add confectioners sugar and process until smooth. Add vanilla and process until well blended. Unroll cooled cake, and spread cream cheese mixture over top of cake. Reroll without towel and place in refrigerator at least 2 hours. Sprinkle with confectioners sugar before serving, if desired.

Strawberry Bread

Long Beach, California
4 to 6 servings

1 package (10 ounces) frozen strawberries in syrup
2 eggs
¾ cup vegetable oil
1¾ cups all-purpose flour
1 cup sugar
1½ teaspoons cinnamon
1 teaspoon baking soda
1 teaspoon salt
½ cup walnut halves

Lightly grease 1½- to 2-quart microproof ring mold or 6-cup brioche pan. Place strawberries in container of food processor and process until puréed. Add eggs and oil. Process until mixed. Stir flour, sugar, cinnamon, baking soda, and salt together and add to food processor with nuts. Process until well mixed. Pour batter into prepared mold and microcook on 50% power 6 to 8 minutes. Increase setting to high and microcook 1 to 3 minutes, or until top is almost dry. Let stand in mold on heatproof surface 10 minutes. Invert onto serving plate.

Tip: Try this bread smothered with whipped cream and fresh strawberries.

Strawberry Party Cake

Merrillville, Indiana
24 squares

1 package (18¼ ounces) white cake mix
1 package (16 ounces) frozen strawberry halves, thawed
1 package (3 ounces) strawberry-flavored gelatin
1 cup boiling water
2 packages (2 ounces each) dessert topping mix

Desserts

Prepare cake mix according to package directions. Spoon into ungreased 13 x 9-inch microproof baking dish and spread batter evenly. Microcook, uncovered, on 70% power 9 minutes, rotating dish one-half turn after 4½ minutes. Increase setting to high and microcook 5 to 6 minutes, or until top of cake is almost dry. Cool in pan on heatproof surface 10 minutes. Drain strawberries and reserve ½ cup syrup. Dissolve gelatin in boiling water and stir in reserved syrup. Punch deep holes in cake with long-tined fork, making even rows across surface and including corners. Spoon gelatin slowly over top of cake. Place in refrigerator to chill. Prepare topping mix according to package directions. Fold in strawberries and spread over cake. Chill until ready to serve. Cut into 2-inch squares.

Tips: Substitute fresh strawberries for frozen and add ½ cup cold water to make gelatin. Substitute whipped cream for dessert topping mix. Refrigerate leftover cake.

Butterscotch Pudding

Grand Junction, Colorado
4 servings

⅔ cup firmly packed brown sugar
2 tablespoons cornstarch
⅛ teaspoon salt
2 egg yolks, lightly beaten
2 cups milk
2 tablespoons butter or margarine
2 teaspoons vanilla

Stir brown sugar, cornstarch, and salt in 2-quart microproof batter bowl or measuring cup. Place egg yolks in medium-size bowl. Add milk and beat to combine. Stir into brown sugar mixture slowly. Microcook on high 6 to 9 minutes, or until microwave thermometer reads 200⁰F when inserted, stirring every 2 minutes. Stir in butter and vanilla. Pour into dessert dishes, cool slightly, and refrigerate until ready to serve.

Pecan Pie

Birmingham, Alabama
6 to 8 servings

1 frozen pie shell, 9-inch
2 tablespoons butter or margarine
3 eggs, beaten
1 cup dark corn syrup
½ cup sugar
1 teaspoon vanilla
½ teaspoon salt
1 cup coarsely chopped pecans or 1½ cups pecan halves
Whipped cream to serve (optional)

Place frozen pie shell in 9-inch microproof pie plate. Microcook on 90% power 1 minute. Mold pie shell gently into pie plate. Prick with fork and microcook on 90% power 4 to 6 minutes, or until light brown spots appear. Set aside. Place butter in 2-quart microproof batter bowl or measuring cup. Microcook on high 30 seconds, or until melted. Add eggs and beat well. Add corn syrup, sugar, vanilla, and salt, and mix well. Arrange pecans in bottom of pie shell. Pour corn syrup mixture over pecans. Microcook on 70% power 8 to 12 minutes, or until knife inserted near center of pie comes out clean. Serve warm or chilled, with whipped cream, if desired.

Funny Fudge

Tulsa, Oklahoma
77 pieces

1 package (16 ounces) confectioners sugar
½ cup butter or margarine
½ cup unsweetened cocoa powder
¼ cup evaporated milk
1 teaspoon vanilla
1 cup peanut butter

Combine confectioners sugar, butter, cocoa, milk, and vanilla in 1½-quart microproof casserole. Microcook on high 3 minutes, stirring after 1½ minutes. Stir in peanut butter. Cool in casserole and cut into 1-inch squares.

Desserts

Chocolate Pie

Columbus, Georgia
6 to 8 servings

Pie Crust

1 cup all-purpose flour
½ teaspoon salt
⅓ cup chilled butter
3 tablespoons ice water

Filling

2 squares (2 ounces) unsweetened chocolate
1 cup sugar
3 tablespoons all-purpose flour
3 egg yolks
1½ cups milk
2 tablespoons butter
1 teaspoon vanilla
2 cups heavy cream, whipped
Semisweet chocolate for shavings

Place 1 cup flour and salt in large bowl. Cut in chilled butter until mixture resembles coarse crumbs. Sprinkle with water, 1 tablespoon at a time, tossing with fork until pastry holds together. Gather into ball, wrap with plastic wrap, and place in refrigerator 30 minutes. Roll out on lightly floured surface to 10-inch circle. Fold into quarters and gently transfer to 9-inch microproof pie plate. Trim edges, fold under, and flute. Prick all over with fork. Microcook on high 6 minutes, or until pastry is dry and flaky, and brown spots appear. Set aside to cool.

Place chocolate in 2-quart microproof batter bowl or measuring cup. Microcook on 50% power 2 to 3 minutes, or until melted. Stir in sugar and 3 tablespoons flour. Beat egg yolks and milk in bowl and add to chocolate mixture. Stir to mix well. Microcook on high about 10 minutes, or until thickened, stirring with wire whisk every 2 minutes. Add 2 tablespoons butter and vanilla, and stir until butter is melted. Pour into cooled crust. Refrigerate until set. Cover with whipped cream and shave chocolate over top.

85

Apple Crisp

Portland, Oregon
4 to 6 servings

5 or 6 apples, peeled, cored, and sliced
1 cup plus 3 tablespoons flour, divided
1 cup granulated sugar, divided
1 teaspoon cinnamon
½ cup firmly packed brown sugar
1 teaspoon baking powder
¼ teaspoon salt
1 egg, beaten

Place apples in 9-inch microproof pie plate. Combine 3 tablespoons flour, ½ cup granulated sugar, and cinnamon, and sprinkle over apples. Cover with vented plastic wrap and microcook on high 3 minutes. Combine remaining 1 cup flour, remaining ½ cup granulated sugar, brown sugar, baking powder, and salt. Toss gently. Add egg and stir until well mixed. Sprinkle over apples and microcook, uncovered, on high 8 minutes.

Deep Dish Apple Crumb Pie

St. Louis, Missouri
6 to 8 servings

1 box (16 ounces) vanilla wafers
¾ cup butter or margarine, softened, divided
5 tablespoons brown sugar, divided
2½ teaspoons cinnamon, divided
½ teaspoon salt, divided
10 medium-size tart cooking apples, peeled,
    cored, and sliced
2 tablespoons all-purpose flour
2 tablespoons lemon juice
1 teaspoon vanilla

Desserts

Place vanilla wafers in container of food processor and process until finely crumbled. Add ¼ cup butter, 2 tablespoons brown sugar, ½ teaspoon cinnamon, and ¼ teaspoon salt. Blend thoroughly and press two-thirds of mixture evenly onto bottom and up sides of 8- or 9-inch microproof pie plate. Microcook on high 3 minutes. Set aside to cool. Mix apples, flour, 2 tablespoons brown sugar, 1 teaspoon cinnamon, remaining ¼ teaspoon salt, lemon juice, and vanilla in large bowl. Spoon into cooled crust and dot with remaining ½ cup butter. Cover with waxed paper tent, and microcook on high 10 to 14 minutes, or until apples are tender. Sprinkle top with remaining crumb mixture, completely covering apples. Sprinkle remaining 1 tablespoon brown sugar and remaining 1 teaspoon cinnamon over crumb mixture. Microcook, uncovered, on high 2 minutes. Let stand on heatproof surface 30 minutes.

Poached Pears with Chocolate Sauce

Aurora, Illinois
4 servings

4 firm pears
3 tablespoons butter
1 square (1 ounce) unsweetened chocolate
¾ cup sugar
¼ cup unsweetened cocoa powder
½ cup half and half
1 teaspoon vanilla

Peel pears, cut in half, and remove cores. Place, cut-side down, in single layer in 11 x 7-inch microproof baking dish. Cover and microcook on high about 6 minutes, or until just tender. Place butter and chocolate in 2-quart microproof measuring cup. Microcook on high 1 minute, or until melted. Combine sugar and cocoa and stir into chocolate mixture. Stir in half and half slowly and microcook on high 1 to 2 minutes, or until bubbly. Stir in vanilla and spoon over pears.

Rhubarb Dream

Des Moines, Iowa
6 to 8 servings

½ cup butter or margarine
5 tablespoons confectioners sugar
1¾ cups all-purpose flour, divided
2 eggs, beaten
1½ cups granulated sugar
¼ teaspoon salt (optional)
3 cups diced rhubarb

Place butter in 9- to 10-inch microproof casserole or pie plate. Microcook on high 1 minute. Stir in confectioners sugar and 1½ cups flour. Press evenly onto bottom of casserole. Microcook on 70% power 5 minutes. Set aside. Place eggs in 2-quart microproof batter bowl or measuring cup. Beat in remaining ¼ cup flour, granulated sugar, and salt. Add rhubarb and stir. Pour into crust and microcook on high 3 minutes. Reduce setting to 70% power and microcook 6 to 9 minutes, or until filling begins to set halfway between center and outside edge of casserole. Place on heatproof surface and let stand until completely set.

Tip: For best results, place dish on microwave trivet during cooking.

Desserts

Fresh Cranberry Bars

Lincoln, Nebraska
6 to 8 servings

¾ cup butter
1½ cups sifted all-purpose flour
1½ cups quick cooking rolled oats
¾ teaspoon baking soda
¾ cup firmly packed brown sugar
2 cups (16 ounces) fresh cranberries
¾ cup granulated sugar
½ cup raisins
4 teaspoons all-purpose flour

Grease 8-inch square or round microproof cake pan. Place butter in 2-quart microproof batter bowl or measuring cup. Microcook on high 1 minute, or until melted. Stir in 1½ cups flour, rolled oats, baking soda, and brown sugar. Mix well. Pat half of oat mixture into bottom of prepared pan. Set aside. Wash and pick over cranberries. Place in 1-quart microproof bowl. Add granulated sugar, raisins, and ½ cup water. Cover with vented plastic wrap and microcook on high 6 to 8 minutes, or until cranberries pop open. Sprinkle with 4 teaspoons flour and stir. Cover and microcook on high 3 to 5 minutes, or until thickened. Spread cranberry filling over oat mixture in pan. Pat remaining oat mixture on top and microcook on high 6 to 8 minutes. Cool in pan on heatproof surface.

Note: Marlene Leising, co-owner of the Lincoln store, wrote *Microwave Cooking — Everyday to Gourmet.* See Marlene's book for lots of great recipes from Lincoln.

7-Layer Cookies

Asheville, North Carolina
6 to 8 servings

½ cup butter or margarine
1½ cups graham cracker crumbs
1 package (6 ounces) chocolate morsels
1 package (6 ounces) butterscotch or
    peanut butter morsels
1½ cups shredded coconut
1½ cups chopped walnuts
1 can (14 ounces) sweetened condensed milk

Place butter in 12 x 8-inch microproof baking dish or medium-size oval microproof roaster pan. Microcook on high 1 minute. Stir in graham cracker crumbs and pat out evenly over bottom of dish. Sprinkle chocolate morsels over crumb mixture. Cover with layer of butterscotch morsels and layer of coconut. Top with layer of nuts. Drizzle condensed milk evenly over layers. (It may look like a lot of milk, but all milk will cook into mixture.) Microcook, uncovered, on high 8 to 9 minutes, or until milk has been absorbed. Let stand in pan on heatproof surface 5 minutes. Cut into squares while still warm. Remove from pan when cool. Store in airtight container.

Granola

Richmond, California
4 servings

6 tablespoons butter
¾ cup quick cooking rolled oats
½ cup whole bran cereal, crushed
⅓ cup whole-wheat flour
⅓ cup raw sugar
½ teaspoon cinnamon
2 tablespoons sesame seed
About 4 cups dried fruit and nuts (coconut, raisins,
    apricots, almonds, sunflower seed, etc.), or to taste

Desserts

Place butter in 2-quart microproof batter bowl or measuring cup. Microcook on high 45 seconds, or until melted. Stir in oats, bran cereal, flour, sugar, cinnamon, and sesame seed. Spread on large flat microproof dish and microcook on high 4 to 5 minutes, or until toasted, stirring every 1½ minutes. Spoon into bowl, add fruit and nuts, and mix well. Store in airtight container.

Tip: Use granola as an unusual and delicious topping for fruit cobblers.

Caramel Corn
Durham, North Carolina

1 cup firmly packed brown sugar
½ cup butter
¼ cup light corn syrup
½ teaspoon salt
½ teaspoon baking soda
1 teaspoon vanilla
3 to 4 quarts popped popcorn*

Combine brown sugar, butter, corn syrup, and salt in 2-quart microproof batter bowl or measuring cup. Microcook on high 4 minutes, stirring after 2 minutes. Stir until blended and add baking soda and vanilla. Place popped popcorn in large brown paper bag. Pour syrup over popcorn and roll top of bag tightly to close. Microcook on high 1½ minutes. Shake bag and microcook on high 1½ minutes. Shake bag and microcook on high 1 minute. Pour onto flat surface, spread out, and allow to cool.

* *Note:* Pop popcorn in microwave corn popper according to manufacturer's instructions. We do not recommend popping popcorn in paper bag because there is very little moisture in popcorn, and bag may ignite. In this recipe, popped popcorn is mixed with a sugar syrup that provides enough moisture to permit safe use of a paper bag for cooking.

Toffee

Highland Park, Illinois

1 cup butter
1 cup sugar
2 chocolate bars (1¼ ounces each)
½ cup chopped pecans

Place butter in 1-quart microproof bowl. Microcook on high 2 minutes. Stir in sugar and microcook on high 6½ minutes, or until toffee is deep caramel color. Pour onto cookie sheet or jelly-roll pan and set aside to cool. When set, pour off separated butter. Break chocolate into small pieces and place in 1-quart microproof measuring cup. Microcook on high 1½ minutes, or until melted. Pour over toffee and spread evenly. Sprinkle nuts over chocolate and let stand until set. Break into serving-size pieces.

Toffee Fondue

Thousand Oaks, California

1 package (14 ounces) caramels
½ cup milk chocolate pieces
¼ cup strong coffee
2 to 4 tablespoons milk
Apple, pear, or banana slices; marshmallows; or
    shortbread; for dipping

Combine all ingredients except dippers. Microcook on high 5 to 6 minutes, or until smooth, stirring every 2 minutes. Serve with assorted dippers.

Index

94

95